FOSTER ASS

RECENT WORKS

Architectural Monographs No 20

FOSTER ASSOCIATES
RECENT WORKS

A.D. ACADEMY EDITIONS / ST MARTIN'S PRESS

Architectural Monographs No 20
Editorial Offices
42 Leinster Gardens London W2 3AN

ISSN 0141-2191

Editorial and Design Team
Andreas Papadakis (Publisher)
Andrea Bettella (Senior Designer)
Vivian Constantinopoulos (House Editor)
Annamarie Uhr, Lucy Baxter, Lisa Kosky

Photography
Richard Bryant; Richard Davies; Dennis Gilbert; Ben Johnson; Ken Kirkwood; Ian Lambot

Publisher's Note
I am grateful to Norman Foster for allowing us to reproduce the edited selection of his writings and lectures, and to Spencer de Grey for his help in the concept and design of the Monograph. Thanks also to Foster Associates, particularly Katy Harris for organising material in this volume. Finally, I am indebted to Kenneth Powell who has not only contributed the Introduction to the Monograph but has also made a substantial editorial contribution in the selection of both projects and writings, and for writing many of the project descriptions.   *ACP*

Cover: Crescent Wing, Sainsbury Centre for the Visual Arts, Norwich; *P2:* ITN Headquarters, London; *P6:* Century Tower, Tokyo

First published in Great Britain in 1992 by
ACADEMY EDITIONS
An imprint of the Academy Group Ltd
42 Leinster Gardens London W2 3AN

ISBN 1 85490 108 7 (HB)
ISBN 1 85490 111 7 (PB)

Published in the United States of America by
ST MARTIN'S PRESS
175 Fifth Avenue, New York, NY 10010

ISBN 0-312-17242-2 (HB)
ISBN 0-312-07146-9 (PB)

Printed and bound in Singapore

CONTENTS

PROJECTS

KENNETH POWELL
INTRODUCTION

'Architecture', Sir Norman Foster has declared, 'is about people and the quality of life . . . Those are the true generators – style and fashion have to be peripheral and secondary'.[1] A few years earlier, however, Foster had admitted that he saw no distinction between architectural design as such and product design, and that he saw a building as 'a product'.[2]

Foster's belief in technological progress is unshakeable – he is an avowed optimist – and he has spoken frequently and eloquently about its influence on his architecture. Yet his view of technological progress is far more down-to-earth and less mechanistic than some of his critics pretend. 'It's not very fashionable to talk about technology,' Foster explained to a Japanese audience last year, 'but I don't see how you can escape making things, and that's what technology is and that's what our culture is.'[3] On many occasions he has spoken of technology in terms of 'making things' and of his practice, Foster Associates, as being concerned above all with the process of making buildings: 'We believe that design is a continuum from the larger total down to the smallest detail and in terms of priority no detail is small.'[4] His notebooks are filled with drawings of heads of screws used to fix glass and bent pieces of metal, alongside some urban masterplan in genesis. Foster expands the credo: 'What excites me is really the ingredients of architecture. It's a bit like being a chef. You don't need expensive materials or grand opportunities to have a feast. And that, I believe, is true of architecture.'[5]

Nearly a quarter of a century ago Norman Foster, along with his late wife and professional partner, Wendy, parted company with Richard Rogers, and Foster Associates was born. The partnership with Rogers had been a happy one and their parting was amicable enough, though times were hard, but the two principals had strikingly different personalities. Rogers is an intensely extrovert figure; the relationship between his personal and professional lives has been memorably expounded by his biographer Bryan Appleyard. Foster, the hard-working perfectionist and fluent draughtsman, was born and educated in Manchester. He rarely talks of his background or private life, yet they are necessarily a part of his make-up as an architect.

Addressing the UIA Conference at Brighton in 1987 – in the midst of the fashion for 'community architecture' – Foster spoke of the area in which he grew up as really a rather rich mix of ingredients. Yes, it was hard and it was poor and it had an outside lavatory; but it also had a corner shop, it had pubs. Visiting Le Corbusier's Unité d'Habitation in Marseilles many years later, Foster found something of this rich mix in a very different setting: the shops were well-stocked, it was clean and there seemed to be a pride in the place.

Foster's early work allowed him to forget his urban roots. His first major independent job, IBM at Cosham, was the model pavilion-in-a-park, one of a series of 'sheds' of which the Sainsbury Centre, Norwich, completed in 1978, was to be the most sublime. A few years before Sainsbury, however, there was Willis Faber, Ipswich, now Britain's only post-war grade I listed building and increasingly recognised as one of the proto-monuments of the New Modernism. Foster sees Willis Faber as a 'profoundly contextual' building completed before Post Modernism made 'context' an obsession – and sometimes an excuse for banality of invention. It also stands as an early harbinger of themes now maturing in Foster Associates' current projects, 'following the medieval geometry rather than creating a window-dressed rectangular box'.

Diversity and history, particularly as they are expressed in the fabric of cities, are themes that Norman Foster increasingly invokes. In the 60s modern architecture, for Foster as for so many others, meant an escape from the failures of the past. For some, it meant erasing the past, and this path led to the commercial megastructure. Foster's work always emphasised quality above quantity: 'Quality is an attitude of mind and it's totally dependent on those people who make things, and if they don't have that respect, then it will show.' There was always, he acknowledges, a strong craft element in his architecture and a respect for materials that is almost Arts and Crafts in its intensity. He sees this as the antithesis of the nostalgic and decadent pastiche of Post-Modern architecture that is currently fashionable.[6] Though he rarely comments on the work of his contemporaries, Post Modernism is clearly, for Foster, not only contrived and ugly but an unhistorical fraud – like the fake Victorian 'white horses' cut into the chalk on the hillsides of southern England, which are figurative, representational images compared with the pure abstract aesthetic of the oldest horses, such as one 3,000-year-old example near his country house in Uffington, Wiltshire.[7]

Foster has had to ponder the 'lessons from the past' (as he describes them) increasingly as the nature of Foster Associates' commissions has changed. From business parks and industrial fringes, they have moved into city centres and locations more sensitive than the 1960s landscape of the University of East Anglia or the fag-end, as it was, pre-Willis Faber, of Ipswich. Burlington House in the West End of London, the ancient heart of Nîmes, the historic, if battered, centre of Frankfurt-am-Main, the banks of the Gironde at Bordeaux, even the abandoned railway goods yard at King's Cross in London – as 'historic' as any of these – are locations that demand a proper sense of place and history.

For Norman Foster history means not a catalogue of details or a strict set of rules, less still a static code of values to be obeyed and revered, but a seamless, continuing process of discovery, inspiration, invention and innovation. Set to work at Manchester University in the 1950s on measured drawings, Foster eschewed the preferred Classical examples in favour of rural windmills and barns – buildings which he still cites as examples of the leading-edge technology of their own day. For a young student it was fascinating to discover that these historic survivals were not just quaint or picturesque, but reflected the over-riding concern of their builders with pure function. He was also fascinated by the urban context – in Tuscan hilltowns, Bath, Oxford and Cambridge, and in London. If there is one unbuilt project that still lingers in Foster's consciousness, it is the BBC Radio Centre in Portland Place, London. 'I have always believed', he declared in his Royal Gold Medal address in 1983, 'that architecture is about people – at one extreme is the private inner sanctum that it can create, at the other extreme are the outside public spaces which are, in turn, created by it. In between such public and private domains, the edges can be consciously or unconsciously blurred.'

Foster quoted the Casbah in Marrakech and Milan's Galleria Vittorio Emmanuele as examples of ways in which that 'blurring' could be achieved. Over the next couple of years the BBC scheme benefited from an intensive programme of research and experiment. Foster was convinced that the scheme answered the needs of London for a reconciliation of public and private, old and new, 'providing a meeting place, a kind of cultural mixing-pot . . . Taking down the barriers and creating an open house, a welcoming place, a fusion'.[8] Its cancellation was a severe blow that still rankles. Some of the ideas behind the BBC scheme – the casbah, the city within a city – found their way into the unexecuted proposals for the Televisa headquarters in Mexico City (1986). They were equally apparent in the entry for the Paternoster Square redevelopment competition (1987). Foster Associates proposed a proudly modern approach to urban design which spurned not only 'pastiche' but equally the more complex and thoughtful gestures to setting and tradition made by James Stirling, Richard McCormac and, indeed, by the competition winners, Arup Associates. In the end, a very different vision of history was to push the plans for the site in a very different direction.

A full ten years before Paternoster, the proposals for the island site at Hammersmith in West London had exemplified a different urban philosophy, reacting to the hostility of the setting by creating an inward-looking building that still bore the stamp of Archigram and the 60s. However, Hammersmith too had been cancelled. Until recently, the image of Foster Associates reflected the enormous impact of one building in particular: the Hongkong Bank. A large model of the Bank stands in Foster Associates' office, close to the table where Norman Foster works. The building – for all its flaws – remains a landmark in his career and in the history of the practice. It is one of the world's great 20th-century monuments. Yet it is an achievement on which Foster is reluctant to dwell, stressing rather the ways in which he and his colleagues learned from and grew from the process of designing and building it. But, in a sense, the Bank was the climax of the first phase of Foster's career, often characterised as being dominated by a concern for technology and structural innovation. But it also embodies values that seem certain to be the key to his work in the 1990s. Foster says that it exemplifies his conviction that 'the design process is partly a search for forms which will humanistically integrate otherwise conflicting needs'. The Bank is primarily a commercial work-place, designed to make the conduct of the activities it contains more efficient. Yet it is also a model for rebuilding a city where high-rise living is inevitable.

The Hongkong Bank certainly confirmed the place of Foster Associates as a truly international office. Practising architecture in Britain during the 1980s was a difficult business. Within a year or two of his Hampton Court speech in 1984, the Prince of Wales had become a point of reference for every architectural issue. Unlike his friend Richard Rogers, Foster refrained from hitting back at the Prince: 'His heart is in the right place,' he wrote.[9] 'The debate is worthy and important . . . But,' Foster added, 'I am fearful of his over-simplistic recipes. They seem to ignore the deeper reality that architecture is but a mirror of social values and technological changes in society at any point in time.' The Prince, in A Vision of Britain, was in due course to pick out Foster's 'brilliantly engineered' designs for the new King's Cross railway terminal for praise. But some of the issues raised in Britain have been a matter for international debate. Post-Modernism had been born out of a public demand for decoration and decorum and played a vital role in the reaffirmation of the art of architecture. The Post-Modernists reclaimed the street and redefined the role of urban building. Norman Foster has never liked the label 'high tech', but there is in his early work a distinct element of celebrating the machine. Now the machine is regarded as at best a convenience, sometimes a foe, and technological advance must be harnessed and controlled. Resources are limited, and human health and happiness are not governed merely by wealth or plenty. A sense of well-being is the outcome of psychological and even spiritual factors. The archetypal 'modern' building, constructed from energy-consuming materials, artificially serviced, at odds with – possibly destructive of – its surroundings and devoid of vernacular reference, seems to support charges that modern architecture is inhuman and unnatural, a passing fancy that society can no longer afford to indulge.

The vision of modern architecture fading away is one which Foster finds as absurd as the idea of technological advances being 'de-discovered'. The technology is there, a potential source of vast benefits to all; it is the way it is used that is wrong. Foster's consistently positive view of technology is, as Chris Abel has pointed out, in tune with the pioneering, ecological approach to architecture of Serge Chermayeff, who was his tutor at Yale and the Briton Christopher Alexander.[10] Foster would argue that his attachment to technology has never veered beyond the bounds of appropriateness. Furthermore, his architecture is traditional in the sense that it uses structure to create space: 'The architecture of the past that I respect seems to be characterised by the creation of spaces to which I can relate and which at the time of their creation either stretched the technology of their day or were within a tradition of making things with a structural integrity.'[11] The great structures of the past employed the most up-to-date technology of their own day; Foster cites Silbury Hill and Chartres Cathedral as awesome achievements of their day. Technology is a part of civilisation, he insists, and being anti-technology is an untenable position akin to declaring war on architecture – and on civilisation itself.

Norman Foster has been relatively reluctant in the past to explore publicly the sources and underlying themes of his architecture, strengthening the superficial impression that the success of his work is the result of a series of accidents or chances. As his architecture enters a new phase in the wake of a series of recently completed and broadly acclaimed buildings, he shows every sign of rethinking, focusing and redefining the themes that have motivated him over the last quarter of a century. In his maturity, he is questioning some of the basic assumptions of the Modernism that has always been at the core of his thinking. He remains very much the central pivot of Foster Associates – an inspiration, a critic, and, increasingly, a team leader who recognises the talents of his colleagues. Foster advances towards the new millennium with a great deal of optimism.

Context and Regionalism – Responding to the Place

'I suppose that the tighter and more challenging the restraints, the more it puts you on your mettle ... There is a proportional return in terms of results,' Foster says of the Sackler Galleries at London's Royal Academy. 'It is a return to a tradition ... a city in microcosm,' he adds. Old and new come together easily and as equals. The scheme, he claims, is rational, optimistic and proud.

At the Royal Academy, conservationists were initially unhappy about plans to remove a second-rate Victorian staircase and doubtful that any sense could be made of the much-altered, long-forgotten garden facade of the old Burlington House. That their doubts have largely been quelled by the completed scheme is the outcome of its fastidious regard for history. The scheme was engendered out of the need to recast the old Diploma Galleries as a secure, well-tempered environment for loan exhibitions. It has materialised as something far more – a rationalisation and replanning of the Academy's aggregation of spaces. Immaculately detailed, it incorporates two core themes of Foster's architecture: light and circulation. The skilful manipulation of natural light has long been regarded as a major element in his art. At Sackler, the light is serene, luminous, incandescent, pouring through the opaque glass of the sculpture gallery and into the 'gap' below through glazed interstices. The galleries make an equally masterly use of daylight, while conservation requirements are provided for by the use of relatively simple technical devices. Circulation at the Academy was a nightmarish confusion for the able-bodied, daunting for the elderly and disabled. The Foster scheme seizes the building's natural assets, including a virtually disused 19th-century staircase of real grandeur, and makes it accessible to all. It rates high amongst Foster's achievements.

Sackler puts to shame the work of lesser designers for whom designing in the context of historic buildings means deference, artifice, 'irony'. Few buildings in Europe are more obviously historic than the Maison Carrée, a Roman temple surviving complete in the heart of the French city of Nîmes. A competition was held in 1984 to design a 'Médiathèque' for a site occupied by a burned-out 19th-century theatre close to this monument. The entries were as varied as the bevy of great names competing. Jean Bousquet, the Mayor of Nîmes, drew up an initial shortlist of twelve, from which four proposals emerged – by Frank Gehry, Jean Nouvel, Cesar Pelli and Foster. Foster's was certainly the most contextual of them, the only proposal that was respectful of the space between the site and the Maison Carrée. Jean Nouvel put the new building below ground, while Frank Gehry's proposal conflicted with the existing lines and heights, and Pelli incorporated the colonnade of the ruined theatre within a curtain-walled box. Foster, it is clear, is no admirer of Deconstructivist tendencies.

The Nîmes Médiathèque, or Carré d'Art as it now tends to be known, represented a new direction for Foster at the time of the competition. The project forced him to come to terms with Classicism at a time when that concept was being brought centre-stage in the so-called 'architectural debate' in Britain. Foster's proposals accepted the grid of the city and provided for a building in a surprisingly formal relationship with the Maison Carrée. Standing on a stone plinth, the building was initially to feature large panels of stone along the elevation facing the famous monument – an un-Fosterish device which attracted some adverse comments. The scheme has gone through three revisions since. In the first, the portico of the old theatre was reluctantly retained. When this device was (to Foster's relief) abandoned, the principal facade was blown wide open, embracing, as it were, the square and drawing people into a central atrium. This began as a passageway through, but developed into something more like the traditional courtyard at the centre of a southern European townhouse – a result of Foster Associates' explorations of Nîmes and its region. In the final scheme, now nearing completion, the courtyard reaches up through the five above-ground storeys of the building, the exterior of which is essentially a composition in glass, clear, opaque and 'fritted'. The influence of Chareau's Maison de Verre, 'discovered' by Foster and Rogers in the late 50s, is obvious. The staircase inside, with glass treads, will be a larger version (up to six metres wide) of that in the Sackler Galleries.

Foster says that Nîmes is traditional almost to the point of being reactionary because it is rooted in the place. Its grand steps and sheltering portico take their cue from the Maison Carrée, and the character of the city saturated the scheme as it evolved. But the building is about the spirit of the past, he insists, with no blurring of the edges between old and new. It is likely to be recognised as one of Foster's supreme achievements to date.

The influence of Japanese architecture is clearly detectable in the Nîmes designs, especially in the screen-like elevations. Foster has been fascinated by Japan since his first visit, admiring its unique blend of a profound traditionalism with an optimistic approach to the radical, the two co-existing with integrity and without apology. Century Tower provided Foster Associates' first chance to build in Japan. The developer, Mr Kazuo Akao, had greatly admired the Bank, and there is a strong element of its structure in the Century Tower. Yet, says Foster, Century Tower is a very Japanese building, and more traditional than many earlier examples of post-war modern architecture in the country, especially in its uncompromising use of natural daylight.

Foster Associates' current work shows a growing willingness to adapt to the *genius loci,* whether the place is central Bordeaux (where the practice has designed a great crescent, on the scale of the Royal Crescent at Bath, in accord with an overall masterplan by Ricardo Bofill), Cambridge or Barcelona. Norman Foster himself seems to be increasingly concerned with history (in his own terms) and with architectural and urban form as a reflection of it. The Stansted Airport terminal is presented in the light of the great Victorian railway termini, the King's Cross masterplan in the tradition of Nash's London. Victorian Britain fills Foster with admiration – its energy, its belief in progress and (increasingly a Foster buzz-word) its optimism. The past is not for him a strait-jacket, but a challenge to be met head-on.

The Greening of Foster's Architecture

Norman Foster has always believed that using good quality, high performance materials in a building makes sense, ecologically as much as financially. Indeed, the effective redundancy and, in some cases, demolition of many cheaply-constructed buildings dating from the development boom of the 1960s underlines the point. Foster Associates have always been associated with an almost obsessional concern for quality: if the right building component does not exist, they will design it and have it made.

Yet both Foster and Richard Rogers rose to prominence through their championing of the machine aesthetic, and Foster's declaration that a building is a product has already been noted. A car or a cooker that is outmoded and outworn is scrapped and replaced. Should not the same fate overtake outworn buildings? Foster was placed in an uncertain position when Willis Faber at Ipswich was listed after its owners announced plans to alter it. While concerned that modern buildings should be adaptable to changing needs, he has not dissociated himself from the preservation order. When the decision was made to extend the Sainsbury Centre, Foster Associates designed a subterranean wing which is deferential to their own earlier work (now a 'historic' building).

Foster Associates' concern for quality extends beyond the surface. Willis Faber marked a revolution in the office environment. The Hongkong Bank Norman Foster sees as a vertical series of clusters of individual 'villages'. He feels angry that so many modern buildings fail the simplest test – they do not work for the people who use them; his formula for Stansted was the pursuit of calm, clarity and convenience, a tonic for air travellers wearied by the visual and organisational confusion of most airports. But he also stresses the degree to which the building, for all its considerable scale, fits into the landscape of rural Essex. The Crescent Wing at the Sainsbury Centre can be linked as much to the desire to protect the landscape as to respect for the adjacent 1978 block.

Foster Associates' masterplan for a derelict industrial area of Duisburg in Germany shows a similar respect for a less auspicious landscape. The Micro Centre, to be built on the site of a demolished factory, is planned to consist of twelve industrial blocks in two 'climate halls'. It is an alternative to the sprawling city-edge business park. The great glazed containers are cooled by air intakes funnelled through banks of trees. The blocks within will have their own servicing.

Ecological concern in architecture is not new – the work of Chermayeff and Alexander has already been mentioned. But ecology is one driving force behind the New Modernism, the exponents of which have turned on their heads many of the precepts of the first Modern age. Will Alsop's thorough-going approach to energy saving helped him defeat Foster in the competition for the new

Hôtel du Département at Marseilles. In a project for a new school at Fréjus – the first the practice has done since the 70s – Foster Associates have taken on board natural ventilation, studying the ingenious devices adopted by traditional Islamic builders to cool structures. Sitting astride a hilltop overlooking the town, the building utilises a 'solar chimney' to draw in cool air on those still, stifling days that can make life uncomfortable in the South. When Norman Foster endorses such 'vernacular' devices, you are reminded of his early enthusiasm for old barns and windmills in preference to Georgian mansions. 'The vernacular isn't quaint or something preserved in aspic,' he says, 'it's on the cutting edge.'

Foster's perennial optimism overcomes any doubts he might have about the future of contemporary industrial society. Recalling, perhaps, the grimy Manchester of his youth, he sees great hope in the new, clean micro-chip based industries of today. But even he now talks about the recycling of materials as a major issue. He invokes the memory of another of his heroes, Buckminster Fuller, who, far from being a dome salesman as some people think, cared passionately about the future of the planet and designed simple, economical buildings. Foster believes that a fine building, made to last, represents a justifiable use of scarce resources (the Rolls-Royce, say, over the Ford Cortina . . .). Foster, interestingly, made no comment when it was announced that the Reliance Controls factory at Swindon (Team 4, 1967) was to be demolished. Richard Rogers commented that it had reached the end of its useful life and wasn't made to last forever. Foster has his doubts about 'throw-away' architecture; however, a structure built to such a demanding specification that it cannot be an economical proposition for the client is an absurdity, especially in the field of commercial architecture. The description of the Hongkong Bank as 'the world's most expensive building' became something of an encumbrance to Foster Associates. Yet the Renault Centre at Swindon cost under £350 a square foot (at 1982 prices) – a typical sum for buildings of its kind. The ITN building, the Battersea office and apartment block, and the recent building at Stockley Park are all examples of relatively economical projects, and a proposed contribution to Stanhope's new office park at Chiswick, West London, will be in the same mould. Foster Associates' Canary Wharf tower, which is unlikely to be constructed until the mid 1990s, was designed to the rigorous prescriptions of Olympia & York. The practice is determined to provide superior commercial buildings at an affordable price.

Nobody, however, looks to the big developers for a lead in producing innovatively ecological buildings. Conventional air conditioning, for example, is usually regarded as one of the points that increase the rental value of a building. The German Commerzbank is, in contrast, an ideal client, committed to high design standards and with a typically German concern for the environment. The Bank currently occupies a variety of buildings across Frankfurt, the most important being a 70s tower block behind Kaiserplatz. The Bank intends to concentrate on this site, replacing its out-stations with a major new building.

Foster's winning scheme provides for a tower on a triangular plan with at its core a slot that runs all the way up the building providing, through the use of fans, a draught of air for natural ventilation of the offices arranged in three 'petals' around it. Every third floor, the offices are interrupted by a garden, three floors high, the gardens being staggered around the three sides of the tower. No office is without a view through a garden and since the gardens and the office floors are suspended in six-storey units from the principal structure, there are no columns to block the views.

The height of the building makes simple opening windows impractical. The office windows do open, but are screened by a further layer of glass which acts as a wind-break. At ground level, the tower has to sit amongst surviving 19th-century buildings. Instead of being a free-standing monument, it is related to them by being set in a courtyard which is covered over to provide a conservatory and restaurant.

Foster Associates' director Spencer de Grey somewhat fancifully imagines kestrels nesting in the trees around the Commerzbank tower – an appealing image of a future where technology and nature are reconciled at last, which embodies the ideal which Norman Foster has been pursuing throughout his career.

Decoration and Poetry

'If the spaces that we create do not move the heart and mind, then they are surely only addressing one part of their function,' wrote Norman Foster recently. Norman Foster's principal early influences were those poetic masters Wright and Le Corbusier. As a young architect he discovered Louis Kahn, who was, he says, a powerful source of inspiration. Kahn's over-riding concern for light and space was taken up and developed by Foster, whose fastidious, sparing approach to structure added another potent ingredient.

Excessive refinement is a characteristic of more than one historic style of architecture in its final, dying phase – the English Gothic of around 1500 is one example. It was the relentless perfectionism of the late work of Mies van der Rohe which prompted Venturi's remark that 'less is a bore'. Mies undoubtedly influenced Foster's earlier work, and the influence was still there in Willis Faber and the Sainsbury Centre. There is a comparable 'classical' quality in Foster's work, though the Hongkong Bank is palpably 'Gothic'. Yet in the best of Foster's more recent works there is a new fluency and expressiveness which provides an alternative to the laboured vulgarity of Post-Modernism and the frenetic contortions of Deconstructivist architecture.

Foster speaks scathingly of the banal repetition of something very ordinary. He scorns the middle ground claimed by architects as different as Robert Venturi and Richard McCormac as tending towards the pursuit of mediocrity. The obsession with being in the middle is, he claims, a depressing, typically British matter of playing to the gallery. Foster does not despise public opinion – though he recognises its malleability and fickleness – and he wants to innovate and lead rather than pander to a perceived demand for a particular way of building.

The Stansted terminal is perhaps the recent work that most fully expresses his vision. The central idea was a clear visual identity, and the form that idea would take was sketched out early in the project. Detailed design work produced the drama and energy of the structural system, which balances the repose of the great glazed container. Above all, there is the quality of light, the outcome of strenuous efforts by Foster and his team. The poetry and the mechanics for Foster are part of the same story: 'If I can get carried away with some passion about the poetry of the light, then I can also in the same vein enjoy the poetry of the hydraulic engineering.'[12] The result is the 'sense of occasion and drama' which he admires in the great Victorian train sheds.

The key element which marks the interaction of the natural and the man-made worlds is natural light, and at the heart of Foster's art is the way in which daylight penetrates buildings and is linked to the system of human circulation. This is as true of a relatively cheap building, like the Stockley Park block, as it is of the Bank or Stansted. Deeply traditional (in the truest sense of the word), technically assured, conscious of history and place, continually striving for a practical form of perfection, Foster's architecture has consistently depended on a mastery of light and space for its success. The richness of invention that produced the Century Tower, Stansted, the Crescent Wing and the schemes for Shinagawa Higashi, the King's Cross terminal and the staggering Millennium Tower is built on this mastery. Norman Foster defines the approach as 'the way you handle something which is essentially simple and give it care and attention . . . so that you transform the whole quality'. Norman Foster's practical poetry is likely to remain a major force in the late 20th-century renaissance of modern architecture because it rejects styling, literary and intellectual allusion, and sheer pretentiousness in favour of the pursuit of excellence.

Notes

All quotations by Norman Foster are taken from an interview between the architect and Kenneth Powell, except where stated.

1 Lecture to Takenaka, Tokyo, March 1990. 2 IDSA Conference, 9 August 1986. 3 Takenaka, 1990. 4 IDSA, 1986. 5 E Lyons Memorial Lecture, RIBA, 1986. 6 *A&U* introduction, 1988. 7 UIA speech 1987. 8 UIA, 1987. 9 Letter to the *Sunday Times*, 6 December 1987. 10 *A&U* Extra Edn, Norman Foster, 1988. 11 Interview with Marc Emery, *L'Architecture d'Aujourd'hui*, February 1986. 12 Tate Lecture, 10 February 1991.

NORMAN FOSTER
SELECTED WRITINGS AND LECTURES

Academy Architecture Lecture

I gave a talk whilst in Japan for the opening of our Century Tower project there, in the course of which I showed a pair of slides that raised the issue of how you bring together the old and the new, the technological and spiritual, and these I symbolised by the computer chip and the Zen garden. It is an issue towards which there is a particular attitude throughout all our work. If function is about keeping the rain at bay and the energy flowing, then it is surely also about the spirit; if you like, the Zen of the project.

Nothing is perhaps so appropriate to the analogy as light. You can measure it, you can quantify it and you can say what is right for a given task. But in the end light and the quality of light in a building or an external space is something far more subjective. One of the themes that weaves itself between our projects over the years is the handling of natural light: how it might inform, diffuse and add another dimension to an interior, whether it's an airport, a building you work in, or a gallery where you look at works of art.

The theme of light was one of the issues raised by the assignment to produce the Sackler Galleries in the 19th-century shell on top of Burlington House. One of the first things that became evident was that it was extremely difficult to access these new galleries. The clue was in the seam line: the area between the original Burlington House and the 19th-century Smirke addition. We had the intention of creating the major new complex of galleries at the upper level, while at the same time attempting to solve the problems of circulation that had beset the Academy for a long time. You couldn't move in any sequential way through the spaces, and you couldn't move works of art easily from the vaults below. The original Diploma Galleries were linked by a staircase and a rather ramshackle lift which Gerald Kelly, the President of the Academy in the 40s, managed to buy from a used-car dealer.

Examining the gap between the buildings we could see just how many little DIY lean-tos had accreted over time. These spaces were 'out of sight, out of mind'; there was no exact information charting them, though you could get a glimpse by opening one of the frosted-glass lavatory windows and peering through. Our aim was to take all that confusion away, cleaning up and restoring those elements and trying to make visually clear which was old and which was a reconstruction. The original Diploma Galleries, which I know were very dear to some people though I don't personally think they were that distinguished, occupied the upper part of Burlington House. Obviously any reworking within that shell would have to respect the cornice line, and that limited any upward growth. We discovered that there was a void that could be used for servicing, so the air conditioning, de-humidification and dust control – all of very high order for these new galleries – were discreetly integrated, taking advantage of the nooks and crannies within the existing fabric.

We wanted the new galleries to have that timeless, coved form appropriate to natural top-lighting, avoiding the problems of shadow. The decision to create a complex of smaller individual rooms was a considered one. We had explored the idea of creating one large space, but it seemed appropriate to create a more intimate grouping of smaller spaces that would more naturally complement the larger ones within the rest of the Academy.

In some of our early model studies of the galleries and the gap between the buildings, the idea developed that a lift could be inserted on one side and that a lot of the very interesting and quite precious rooms could actually be opened up. Before this work was undertaken the Reynolds rooms, for example, had permanent shutters and no connection with the outside. The possibility of getting top light down the crack between the original Burlington House, of peeling back time to the end of the last century, was very appealing. It would reveal the Samuel Ware elevation and the 19th-century elevation to the main building, which had never seen the light of day.

The knitting together of spaces outside the gallery – the circulation staircase, the lift and the Michelangelo Tondo – all came out of an extraordinary chemistry that developed with Arthur and Jill Sackler. Both displayed a wonderful drive – impatience is perhaps too strong a word – and a marvellous sense of endeavour and vision to take a broader view of the total. I'm sure that there are individuals and institutions that make purely financial contributions to the arts, but the important thing here was that the Sacklers also had a tremendous creative input.

The idea of using glass in staircases and in floors is really quite an old one. Pavement lights are an integral part of historic London, so in using sand-blasted glass we were really exploiting elements special to a given point in time, which give the city its vibrancy, its diversity. The glass which provides the side-lighting in the sculpture gallery required extraordinary endeavours to achieve that degree of whiteness. Its translucence is reminiscent of the Shoji screens of earlier Japanese architecture. The interlayer enables natural light to pour in, giving it that luminosity and also allowing the possibility of backlighting the wall from the other side so that it glows at night. Only in Czechoslovakia were we able to find a glass of such purity that it was totally white, without any 'greenness'.

Each age produces its own vocabulary, has its own integrity and makes its own mark. I am quite sensitive to the fact that this is currently an unfashionable view of how you bring the old and the new together, but it is an approach which has been quite fundamental to our thinking.

The proposals for the new Carré d'Art are inspired by the Roman grid of Nîmes. It seemed to us that there was a powerful generator in its spirit. Rather than trying to ape the trappings of a Roman era, it seemed logical to take the typical Roman grid block and to fill it to the edges, respecting the square in front of it. It seemed important to us to respect the height-lines of the adjoining buildings and to work within them, to continue the grain of the city.

The decision to create a courtyard at the heart of that building was in its own way reminiscent of a lot of Nîmes historic architecture in which buildings deep within the blocks are penetrated by individual courtyards. We were also aware of that tradition of stepped routes through the hill-towns in the region. It was out of that background that the scheme evolved as essentially a low building. It was also rather like a ship in that those areas concerned with 'driving', servicing and storage would be well below ground and those areas that would need natural top light would, quite logically, find their way to the upper reaches.

It was a building that would bring together two cultures: that concerned with the visual arts and that concerned with information. The médiatèque building would act as a short cut from the main route through the building, on the diagonal, to a minor entrance at the rear. This well travelled route connects the principal monuments in Nîmes: from the Roman amphitheatre through to this square, the Maison Carrée and then beyond to the water gardens of Le Nôtre.

The building was conceived as having a very large portico that would provide weather protection for an upper-level café overlooking the square. Then by 'biting' into the corner we would create a primary entrance. This is a modest building with simple exposed concrete structures at six-metre centres; you really can't do anything more economically or directly in that particular part of France.

There is a transition in the development of the building. Over the later phases we decided it would be more appropriate to break the scale down on the edge, to create an inner grain in front of the main concrete structure. The basement wall adopts a curve on plan to protect the very ancient tree on the corner, which is really quite an important ingredient. The steel column on the corner was almost literally threaded through the tree to relate the two together. The Carré d'Art takes the very simple ingredients of a concrete structure, stretching and refining them, and using the steel elements in a conscious dialogue between the square and the historic building which sits within it, but totally removed in time.

The interplay between past and present also took place at King's Cross, where our masterplan aimed to unify the currently separate stations of King's Cross and St Pancras. The central features of this would be a 25-acre park and, at the southern end, a new railway terminal related to the channel tunnel. London has its own characteristics quite different from those of grid cities such as Paris, New York, Barcelona, Amsterdam or Washington. London is really a collection of green spaces, some large and some small; they roll off the tongue – a London bus or any map will identify Shepherd's Bush, Islington Green, Hampstead Heath; the list is endless. These special places, each with its own character, seemed to us the essence of London.

Our proposed new park is penetrated by Regent's Canal and takes up the spirit of London's past to create the first major park since the last century; to reinstate the waterway which had been largely concreted over by later transportation systems; and to effect a relationship between the existing historic buildings, preserving the best of them. We aim to develop a dialogue between the hard-edged urban water of a canal, an excavated waterbasin, and the soft water that you might associate with a lake, nature reserve or park. We tried not to be seduced into designing buildings, but instead to suggest what might be appropriate to the site in terms of massing and enclosures.

We drew comparisons with London's prime existing streets, comparing our proposals for a major north-south boulevard with Regent Street and hoping to incorporate arcades. Having suggested this framework, we wanted to burst through the insularity, prejudice and petty-mindedness that exists in this country. We intended to have architects from Europe, Japan and America doing individual buildings. This is something that so far has not happened in this country – our insularity is really a disgrace, especially when you consider the opportunities that Europe and Japan have opened up to architects from Britain. Although the scheme is being negotiated with the planners there is the potential to bring together a very committed and interesting group of people.

It is a project generated by the very powerful geometry of the two historic stations of King's Cross and St Pancras. Our building demonstrates how a structure can respond to the site, create a coherent route and also flood the interior with natural light, in a very controlled way.

I believe the original layers of history in a building are made far more real when they are seen alongside the new. The same thing also happens in reverse: you need be in no doubt of what is of this age. This is something we have become blind to, taking it for granted that the richness of so many of our cities comes about because each age has had the confidence to make its own stamp in an optimistic and forward-looking manner.

This is really the preamble to our work at Stansted airport. Airports, we realised, have none of the sense of occasion and drama that we associate with the great train stations. It seems that an earlier age had a confidence and a romance with their form of transportation. We felt that we should strive to bring some of that sense of occasion to air travel and to somehow raise the spirits in an airport so that it does not have to be what we have come to regard as a very dreary, pressured experience.

Another issue at Stansted was the environmental impact of putting a large-scale terminal on what would be a green-field site but for a World War II airstrip for heavy bombers; a major design implication was how to respect the tree line in this very rural setting.

We felt it would be interesting to go back and to look at the roots of air travel. In the earliest airfields you were in no doubt where you were. You walked towards the aircraft and when you returned you walked towards the road (or more likely a dirt track). There was a clear airside and landside; you didn't need complex signing systems. Even though the realities of security and immigration would not allow that directness of experience, we wanted to avoid the confusion created as large international airports grow over time, on restricted sites.

By shedding those inhibitions of the past we hoped to see what opportunities might exist and to question how a building like this might be serviced, whether it really made sense to build structures that would not only hold the roof up but also support brick-built structures around air conditioning that negated any possibility of natural light.

The result of that questioning was summed up in our earliest models, which took advantage of a fall in the site by digging in a two-storey building, creating the illusion on the landside of a single storey building in which people could move at one level without any changes of direction. The essential idea was to create a large room whose structure would be primarily concerned with holding up a roof that could let in natural light in an energy-efficient way. Such a structure could also modulate and give a sense of scale to the space. At the same time we had to meet some of the more down-to-earth aspects of the brief: security, through-put and baggage handling. A major factor in the brief was to reduce the cost of the terminal. Stansted was more than ten percent cheaper than comparable terminals at Gatwick and Heathrow, depending on how you examine the figures.

In our early plans the submerged undercroft contained all those heavy elements that normally sit on the roof, as well as the baggage-handling facilities, while the people would be above because you enter an aircraft at the upper level. The idea was to create something that might have the flexibility for change in an industry which is extraordinarily volatile.

The undercroft now has a full-scale mainline railway station that came in during the early stages of the construction, and the same flexibility allowed for a road through the building, which meant that the shorter-life servicing equipment could be moved.

The very large roof will grow in a linear way: its first phase catering for eight million people a year and the final form for 15 million. It is made up of a series of vaults and is very much about the qualities of natural light. Endless calculations ensured a shaft of sunlight could penetrate to produce a highlight on the floor. Daylight reflectors suspended below the rooflights would avoid the experience at night of looking up at a black hole, as a white perforated panel would admit light in a diffused way and cut down the heat gain, while acting as a kind of sculptural element within the shape itself. The roof is really about light and water, and all the heavy equipment is at the bottom. Banished are those ugly exposed ducts and diffusers, and fluorescent lights and ceiling tiles.

If the structure is a conscious element to give order – to offer a view of aircraft to which you are beckoned notwithstanding the proliferation of security and baggage screens – it is also a means to communicate information on flight times and so on. The poetry of the lighting is for me matched by a different kind of poetry, and that is the hydraulic engineering which allows you to drain water from a space roughly the size of six football pitches and pull it to the edges, maintaining the hierarchy between the structure which is holding up the building and the structure which is holding up those membranes on the outer edge, some of which are translucent on the sides. The use of conventional roof drainage would have had massive implications. I find a certain elegance in the way we have used stainless steel pipes which run absolutely flat in the roof. A traditional system would have meant something like two metres between the upper reaches of the roof and the lower reaches around the gutters. Our system starts from the idea that you don't create columns of air with only a thin layer of water around the outer edge but that you create a smaller tube, which when it really does rain is chop-full of water, and it has proved really quite remarkable in its use. On the edge of the roof are the equivalent of the spoilers on a large jet, which break down the air flow, avoiding the problems of uplift in high winds. During construction it withstood an extraordinary battering in freak gales.

The questions of natural lighting so crucial at Stansted were also fundamental to the Sainsbury Centre. In the original building of 1978 the key ingredient was a flexible top-lit space that would integrate a wide variety of activities: those to do with viewing art and studying art history, as well as a restaurant, faculty club and so on. It was constructed to be open-ended for future growth, and it is in the spirit of the cave and the tent that the Crescent Wing expands the original building discreetly in the landscape, its through views remaining unchanged. What is difficult to comprehend is that the new extension is something like two-thirds the footprint of the original building.

The two projects are complementary but also quite different. The Crescent Wing, with its very large roof and its earth cover, is very much in the spirit of earlier roofs such as Willis Faber, and going back even further, the Creek Vean house in the 60s.

The glass-covered ramp which gives public access to these facilities goes down to a triangular gallery space which is well equipped for conferences, with very good audio-visual facilities. It also descends to a storage area of which, as far as I am aware, the only other example is in the Metropolitan. Here a member of the public or a scholar can access all the works of art contained in the building, unlike the typical museum or gallery where the storage area is a vast private domain.

The triangular gallery also has a system of flexible lighting, so that for the first time it will be possible to teach lighting as a subject. Even though it is an underground building we have incorporated natural top lights as well as the dramatic sweep of glass inset into the landscaped slope from which the Crescent Wing derives its name. The top-lighting takes the form of a curved strip which marks the ramp down to the main hall, and discs over parabolic reflectors to the laboratories below. These are literally set flush with the grass to leave the main view from the original centre unchanged.

I would like to continue this theme of natural lighting with the Hongkong Bank. In the Banking Hall one can see sunlight on the cross bracing and on the glass underbelly that visually connects the main public space with the public route below it. That public route is enhanced by sunlight which is pulled in by a system of mirrored reflectors or 'sunscoop' as it is known. Even on overcast days there is a quality of light here which is different from a totally internal space. It was an opportunity to explore an alternative to the anonymity and the repetition of the typical office building.

Conditions in Tokyo are similar to those in Hong Kong in that the city suffers hurricanes, but unlike Hong Kong, Tokyo also has to cope with earthquakes, and this has very real implications for structural design. One of the many early study sketches for our Century Tower project explored an idea with an orthogonal structural grid on the sides and a raked geometry creating double-height spaces and offering a rich mix of spaces for the market. We were working with a client who was enthusiastic about breaking down some of the barriers between public and private by creating an art gallery, residential area, swimming-pool, club, restaurant, tea-house and public meeting point, and examining whether some or all of these could come together in a building with very different codes and a restricted site.

It was a building that anticipated a degree of growth, and showed an awareness of changing legislation that might allow more relaxed light angles. Mindful of that, the building was conceived as two towers with a light shaft between them. The idea was that they could grow quite independently, as and when the legislation changed. What actually happened was that at a very late stage in the design, the legislation did change and so the building did expand during the design phase. The services, lifts and staircases are pulled to the sides so that working spaces are very much about sun and view, and those prime views look right out to the city beyond. There is an interesting linkage here between the above- and below-ground experience of space. The offices which relate to a vertical shaft of light are now fully let and the combination of single and double heights offers quite a rich mix. The above-ground building is linked with the experience below ground by continuing the space, making the staircase that takes you to the galleries below the major element and also linking you across to the glass pavilion which is at the rear of the site, enclosed by a wall. An important ingredient is water, with reflecting pools at the base of the wall and water cascading as a flowing film over the granite. There is a striving for a greater richness and diversity of experiences, and the pool and its catenary structure of glass and louvres further extends the vocabulary of space.

The building works in a special way at night; giving a very distinctive expression of the structure. Many Japanese commentators have expressed opinions about the way it evokes certain characteristics of traditional Japanese architecture.

In Barcelona there was a different kind of assignment, the outcome of an international competition for an Olympic communications tower on a prominent site on top of the mountains that overlook the city. This is a project about many important things; it is a symbol for the city, but it is also about pollution – visual pollution. The mayor, in an extraordinary civic initiative, said that it was completely out of the question that Telefònica, Spain's equivalent of British Telecom, Spanish and Catalan television should each build their own tall tower. But the idea that these rivals would form one company which would realise and operate the tower seemed quite inconceivable. The Ayuntemiento, the City Hall, were also saying that they should have a minority interest in the company, and just to rub salt into the wounds, demanded that the tower should have a viewing platform to allow the public another perspective of their city, despite the extreme problems of security this would entail.

The removal of a mass of illegal masts, antennae and dishes and their grouping on one new mast was very much an environmental issue. The site is a national park, which certainly compounded the problem, so our aim was to make the slenderest possible intervention, taking a totally new look at the nature of a communication mast.

Traditionally these masts are concrete structures, but in scribbles done just before the meeting with the competition jury, we showed that such a mast on this site would have to be a massive 25m wide at its base, the equivalent, if you like, of a brick chimney. We wanted to get that minimum, most slender element and then to guy it with cables. The technology is really very straightforward, the kind of thing you would associate with suspension bridges.

The related communications building was buried and turfed over and the mountain eventually put back around it. The tower will be almost 300m in its final form. The 13-storey structure of platforms, which is the equivalent of 25 storeys of a domestic building, and weighs something like 30,000 tonnes, was hoisted up the concrete core. That core is the most basic way that you can move services vertically. It is the thinnest possible pipe, and works rather like a car aerial with two further structures at the top which will slide out telescopically. The final top section, a bit like the droop-snoot on a Concorde, is a crane that can angle and then traverse so that it can move the dishes which will change constantly during its life. The construction started in February 1990 and will be completed by the summer of 1991.

It would be very difficult to talk about buildings and structures without talking about how they are put together. I think the label 'hi-tech' is in all kinds of ways questionable, and I have never really understood it. It's almost as if this age has technology and no age in the past did. If you go 5,000 years back over time, an earth mound like Silbury Hill is an extraordinarily sophisticated structure 130 feet high, and undoubtedly at the cutting age of that technology, just like the pyramids, the Alexandria lighthouse of 30 BC, the great cathedrals of the middle ages, and the explosion of industrial construction at the beginning of the 19th century. Technology is something that has been there throughout time, and those structures which have endured or which command attention are always on the cutting edge, stretching the boundaries of technology, and taking to the ultimate the art of making things.

I would like to conclude by remembering two men who are symbolic for all these projects. One is the individual who headed the Swiss team responsible for physically raising the 30,000 kN platform in Barcelona. He symbolises those craftsmen who make the buildings. Even though the building site has more and more become the assembly point for prefabricated elements, it still does not mean that craftsmanship and pride have been replaced by robots – the tools might be different but quality is still determined by the attitude and motivations of people. Finally, the other individual is the mayor of Barcelona. He symbolises the patron – the prime mover – in many respects he is the true architect of the tower because without his initiative, continued commitment and support it would never have happened. Of course I should also mention Jill and Arthur Sackler, Sir Robert and Lady Sainsbury, Sir Norman Payne . . . it is a long list. But then the story of architecture is the story of patronage.
(*Lecture at The Royal Academy, London, June 1991*)

The Microchip and The Zen Garden

In the past, I have used the two images of an enlarged microchip alongside the Zen gravel garden at the Ryoanji Temple in Kyoto to make points about our work.

In Japan more than anywhere else, there is a culture where the old and the new coexist – with integrity and without apology. These two images contrast and complement each other; and they also symbolise a personal attitude to the way in which the new and the old come together.

This attitude permeates our every project, whether it is the conversion of a historic building, or the insertion of a new structure into the urban fabric of an ancient town, or a masterplan for growing and regenerating an existing city. In such an approach, every age makes a mark and has its own identity. In one sense there is a break with the past, but that is in itself a powerful and long-standing tradition. Continuity is inherent in the spirit of the new.

These two images also make a point about function. The 'chip' symbolises the flowing of energy within systems. It symbolises a building or a city in microcosm, with systems for the flow of water, waste, air, electricity, information, people, cars, trains, aircraft. . . But that objective, quantifiable side of the equation is only one part of the function. What about the subjective, the needs of the spirit? Why are crowds attracted to certain places and spaces? Why do we stand in awe of a rectangle of gravel? Why are we arrested by the sweep of an arch in a cathedral?

If the spaces that we create do not move the heart and mind then they are surely only addressing one part of their function.

Light is a good example. Any engineer can quantify and produce enough light with which to brighten a passage or by which to read a book. But what about the poetic dimension of natural light: the changing nature of an overcast sky, the discovery of shade, the lightness of a patch of sunlight?

This is the theme we explore in our room at the Venice Biennale.

(*Text for the Venice Biennale, September 1991*)

The Politics of Infrastructure

In 1953, when you could travel across the Atlantic by the propeller-driven Constellation in up to 20 hours, Stansted was identified as London's potential third airport. Nearly 40 years later, after three public inquiries, three committees, four reports, one review and one false start, the new International Terminal at Stansted has at last been officially opened. Compare this with the creation of Charles de Gaulle airport in Paris.

A green field at Roissy was identified in 1958 as the site. 15 years later, Charles de Gaulle was opened. Examining these two airports is not to compare like with like, because Charles de Gaulle was a massive new undertaking, carrying 22 million passengers in 1990, while Stansted is built around a single World War Two runway. In other words, the advantages were all in Britain's favour. So the time difference between the two ventures gives rise for even greater concern.

Can we justify those 30 wasted years and is this an isolated example? Sadly not, in either case; delays and deliberations have become a national way of life here. Not only are they frustrating and demoralising: they are indulgently expensive. The public processes take so long that the real issues become even more obscured over time and the conditions prevailing quite different.

We have deceived ourselves into believing that bureaucracy is democracy. We rest on our crumbling laurels, mostly inherited from l9th-century forebears. But unlike them we have little civic pride in the present.

Instead we nostalgically hanker for the glory, more imagined than real, of a time past. We resist change, often in the guise of indiscriminate conservation. I wonder whether the experience of a more enlightened and progressive Europe will shock us into realising how badly we treat ourselves and how far our standards have fallen behind.

Cross the Channel and you will find that things happen more quickly and in a far more civilised fashion. There is a forward-looking optimism matched with a sense of social urgency – it manifests itself in public debate and in a culture of new buildings for public use – galleries and museums for the arts; halls for leisure; stadiums for sport.

Compare London with Paris. It would be impossible to find the equivalents of the remodelling of the Louvre, the Centre Pompidou, the Palais Omnisports de Paris, the Grande Arche and the new Palais de Congrès International, a £150 million investment next to the Eiffel Tower. One could draw similar parallels with many other European cities. Then consider how quickly these projects are realised, even though they are subject to open design competitions. The Centre Pompidou, from first proposals to its opening, took six years. The Palais Omnisports took six years and the Palais de Congrès will take four years.

Contrast our own sad record of stop-go for major projects. This year, the Hampton site extension to the National Gallery will open 43 years after the idea was first proposed. In 1996 the new British Library will open 34 years after its inception. Even Wren, despite all the indignities that he suffered, managed to realise St Paul's Cathedral in that length of time.

Architecture is just part of a much bigger problem. It is about long-term investment rather than short-term expediency, investing in the well-being and education of future generations as well as caring for the present. It is about the quality of life – all the factors which determine whether a society flourishes or declines, whether a city is a European capital attracting outside investment or a regional, inward-looking metropolis. It is significant that the United Kingdom is right at the bottom of the European league in its level of investment on infrastructure. We could learn much from our own history. The entire 10,700 mile National Intercity Network that we possess today was in place by 1849, only 20 years after the first passenger railway opened for business. In 1840, at the height of the railway boom, 299 Railway Bills were passed through Parliament – an average of one every 1.2 days. Compare this with the five years that it recently took to pass the single Act of Parliament to allow the start of the one-and-a-half mile tunnel to link the terminal of the Dockland Light Railway to Bank Underground Station.

Unlike our pioneering rail network, our motorway system is a national disgrace – always too little and inevitably too late. It took four years to build the 16-mile Warwick link to complete the M40 motorway, 18 years after it was first proposed.

Before you can design anything from the humblest building to the most extensive masterplan, you must be able to relate to a decision-making body with clear lines of communication.

If that is true in the microcosm of an architectural practice, then it is mirrored on a larger scale in the procedures that communities adopt to renew the fabric of their towns and cities. It is the quality of that interaction, the level of patronage, political will or absence of it, that will determine the quality of the environment. It is very much about leadership and attitudes of mind. We do not have to be the victims. We should redesign the processes.

I could quote first-hand experience with innumerable mayors and civic leaders across the breadth of France, Spain and Germany, in cities and small towns alike, all having the pulse of their communities, all tireless in their efforts to promote long-term works for future generations. Such people are political figures, household names, as well known and, in their own way, as capable of arousing popular passions as footballers. It is ironic that many of these mayors use design and planning skills from this country; for example, our own office has a working relationship with a dozen across Europe. These are people with a mandate for action – exactly the kind of individuals who should be structured to lead our own cities and towns – the opposite of our chain-bearing civic mascots. Consider the plight of London – it would be difficult to think of a metropolis more in need of this kind of leadership.

Such local initiatives start from the top. In France, for example, the President involves himself personally in design competitions for major projects for both public and private sectors. This approach percolates right through French society.

I sometimes wonder if there is a connection between the breakdown of civic pride and our lack of respect for those involved in the making of things. This tendency is reflected in the positive balance of trade in manufactured goods we maintained from the 18th century until 1983, when it dropped into deficit for the first time. You can see these trends clearly in an analysis of the make-up of our British projects compared with our work in Japan and Europe. Here, depending on its complexity, a typical commercial project would have a dependency of between 25 percent and 33 percent on imported goods. Significantly these would be manufactured elements with high unit goods; prefabricated components like air conditioning units, wall cladding and roofing systems. Whereas our typical Japanese or European project would have only four to five percent of imported elements. An analysis of the reality behind these figures will reveal an even bleaker picture.

It is a bit like that old story about a pilot arriving in New Zealand who informed his passengers that they would be landing shortly and suggested that they set their watches back 30 years. In the l9th century, the railways brought unified time to Britain; before that each city and town had a different time. Will we learn from our past and our European neighbours or will the future train driver emerging this side of the Channel Tunnel be cautioning his passengers to prepare for a 30-year time difference?

(*Article in* The Daily Telegraph, *March 1991*)

Architecture and the Art of Making

At the risk of stating the obvious, I would suggest that architecture is about people and the quality of life. I'm not suggesting that architecture can achieve that in isolation, but I feel that those are true generators – style and fashion have to be peripheral and secondary. It's not very fashionable to talk about technology, but I don't see how you can escape making things, and that's what technology is and what our culture is. It's not fashionable, but I think it has to be confronted nonetheless, because architecture which is created, is rooted in the past but is generated by present needs; it must anticipate a future in which the only constant is change. I'm fascinated by the technological changes and some of the shifts away from the labour-intensive production line which are geared to repetition; the transformations following from those changes, that shift from the heavy batch production which so typifies the 60s in terms of those repetitive, heavy point blocks which stand uniformly across the landscape of Europe and elsewhere. In the shift to the white-collar, non-labour-intensive, responsive and flexible technologies, I enjoy the way that Stafford Beer in the 60s talked about that heavy, repetitive production line as the only way in which corporations could survive, by paying advertisers huge sums of money to make less mutable an environment to which the individual organism cannot adapt. If the dinosaur can no longer live in the world, the world must be turned into a dinosaur sanctuary, which may well explain why some of those buildings have to come down and be replaced by environments which are more human and put much more emphasis on the quality of life.

It seems that with the microprocessor, and its ability to adapt to individual projects instead of tuning the consumer to the machine, it is now possible to tune the machine to the consumer – and that's a shift from the consumer being the servant to being the master. But only if we choose to harness it, and I find a certain irony here that is out of fashion, not only in the practice of architecture but in the architectural schools – if you can't understand the production how can you harness it and move forward in an optimistic way?
(*Extract from Lecture, Takenaka, Tokyo, 1990*)

Architecture and Structure

For me, the history of architecture is the history of the evolution of structures and services. We wouldn't be able to sit here protected from the rain if there wasn't a structure that held this up. And we would certainly not be in a fit state to continue this dialogue if it wasn't for those things that we take for granted in terms of the ability of this space to be serviced. The structure is manifest, it's not worn like a label; it explains the way the building is put together, and demonstrates a lot of the quality and care that have gone into that. It's evolved and changed over time, it breaks down the scale of the spaces, it offers a richer experience, and it works visually as well as structurally. For the buildings that evoke a response in me that I admire and enjoy – wherever they are in the world – the structure has been a key ingredient in the form, appearance, the way that that building would affect me.

That is true of a lot of indigenous buildings in the tradition of Rudofsky – architecture without architects – because there was somebody designing them and making them. They were responding to the climate, they were responding to the materials in a very human way. And in some small part, I think of what we do as an attempt to somehow rediscover some of those traditions. In that sense, the experience of working with kindred spirits of different skills is very much an integral part of the process of designing.
(*Extract from Lecture, Foster 10 Exhibition, Century Cultural Centre, Tokyo, June 1988*)

The Spirit of Architecture

I find the clarity of Sir Henry Wooton's description of architecture in 1624 as 'Firmness, Commodity and Delight' quite refreshing in the light of all the current architectural *isms* – especially its emphasis on people and their needs for *convenience* and *delight*. Despite the shifts of social and technological change which have been explosive in the last three hundred years, the goals suggested by this description still seem to me to be as valid as ever.

It is important that there are no misunderstandings about my own motivations. I practise architecture for the pleasure that I derive from its pursuit – even if, at times, the disciplines and demands seem insuperable. To paraphrase Charles Eames, I like to think that I take my pleasures seriously. In that spirit I should also mention aviation – not for the occasional pleasure that it gives me but because I believe it offers experience and analogies which I can inform the world of architecture. As Bucky might say, there is for me a synergetic relationship between the two. I am more at home designing than talking about design, so I shall mostly be referring to our own work to identify beliefs and attitudes, how they have changed over time and how they are still developing. I shall try to resist the temptation to post-rationalise and shall make an effort to communicate a reality which, for me, owes a great deal to pragmatism and intuition.

I have always believed that architecture is about people – at one extreme is the private inner sanctum that it can create, at the other extreme are the outside public spaces which are, in turn, created by it. In between such public and private domains the edges can be consciously or unconsciously blurred, to create or modify communities by sustaining, erecting or breaking down social barriers. Such an approach involves value judgements by attempting to ask the right questions – it suggests an interactive process between those who initiate buildings, those who use them, and those who design them – another way of saying teamwork.

It implies challenge. Such a process may confirm the status quo, may merely be an audit which rubber-stamps an existing model as appropriate for duplication. On the other hand it may lead to building forms that are different, that are breaking with a current tradition, creating fresh possibilities or harking back to an earlier tradition. It assumes research and an ordering of priorities. In broadbrush terms, such an approach may suggest fragmentation, the creation of several parts rather than one monolith. Alternatively, the process might lead to integration, the creation of one entity rather than separate parts. In fundamental terms it might even question the wisdom of doing a building at all, or suggest thresholds of appropriateness.

It has more to do with optimism than pessimism. It is about joy, and may be sustained by illusion (the illusion of order in a disordered world, of privacy in the midst of many, of space on a crowded site, of light on a dull day). It is also about quality – quality of space and the light that models it.

At some point it involves making a building and unless we return to the cave it raises the issue of technology, 'the art of making things', to quote Pirsig, the production process as a means to an end. I believe quality, that quality of loving care if you like, has always been a preferred ingredient and is needed more today than ever before. Architecture exists in a timeframe. It cannot be separated from the past; intangible earlier influences and reference points. But architecture exists quite firmly in the present and assumes an attitude to the future and change. Lastly it cannot be created in a vacuum. The forces which create it are only sustained by resources – time, energy and funds. I should add one further word concerned with the learning curve – those perceived failures, or satisfactions, expected or otherwise – let's call it feedback.

(*Extract from the Royal Gold Medal Address, RIBA, London, June 1983*)

Design For Living

There is a tendency for a certain mystique to develop around such words as 'design', especially 'good design'. This is unfortunate because it tends to cloud the importance that design decisions have in our lives. Virtually everything that is man-made has been subject to a design process involving deliberate choices and decisions; in our Western civilisation that means nearly everything that we see, hear, touch and smell. As in all things this is something that we can do well, badly or indifferently with corresponding end results. To this extent the very quality of our day-to-day living is profoundly influenced by the quality or our design.

Our environment is a compound of many tangible objects and enclosures whose designers may be anonymous, often hidden in bureaucratic and business organisations, or sometimes independent consultants. Their main role, in essence, is problem-solving. It is this fundamental aspect of their work which is so often overlooked.

The 'style' in which the problem is solved is far less important and it is unfortunate that this aspect is often over-emphasised. This dilemma can be seen in two current attitudes. First, there is a public apathy and indifference to the most fundamental aspects of design as they affect our very existence. Second, there is a tendency among designers to over-indulge in the more superficial aspects of their trade to the exclusion of the fundamental problems. The ensuing dialogue with its overtones of 'good taste' and mystique is largely irrelevant to a world going about its business.

As a random example of the above dilemma it is worth considering the 'tower block' of flats in the form which is currently designed and built in Britain. As a design for a family with young children it is chronically unsuitable. Despite all popular conceptions it is not the only way to achieve high densities; students of architecture were drawing-up low-rise, high-density schemes six or seven years ago. Nevertheless, it is commonplace for architects and critics endlessly to debate at the level of imagery and detail those 'tower blocks' which are 'good' and those which are 'bad'. Obviously some are better than others at a superficial level, but fundamentally a tower block is a tower block, regardless of whether it is Neo-Georgian, mock-Tudor or plastic-faced.

It is amazing how long outdated design concepts can survive. At least our housing has attempted many new forms and experiments since the Industrial Revolution. By comparison, our design for industry has been virtually at a standstill since the 1800s. We still persist in building management 'boxes' and workers' 'sheds' even though this may actually conflict with the needs of processes, expansion, flexibility and management policies.

Obviously, some types of industries and processes are still rooted in a 'clean and dirty', 'we and they' social structure, but they are a growing exception. The traditional factory building and so-called industrial estate is currently one of our most unpleasant, uncomfortable, inefficient and expensive hangovers from the past.

These examples are only part of a totality. The family living in the tower block may be 20 miles from a major airport but deafened by one of its flight paths, traffic jams may separate the worker's factory from home, other facilities such as shopping, schools and recreation may be similarly unrelated. It is an indictment of our educational system that we accept such patterns almost without question as the mythical price of progress and frequently continue to regard good design as 'arting-up' or cosmetic treatment that can be applied 'after the act'.

At the risk of over-simplification, the designer's task could be summed up as analysing set problems in the widest sense and organising the best available resources to achieve the highest-performance solution in the most economical manner. It follows that the end result will have accommodated and integrated often conflicting and competing requirements. The very core of the problems and the way they are resolved will largely generate the style.

It should not be thought that so fundamental an approach is insensitive to the full range of our spiritual and material needs. Most of the historic places which today still continue to delight us were originally a calculated response to well-defined requirements.

For example, Bath was a speculative developers' 'New Town', based on a simple structural system of repetitive cross walls and repeated narrow window openings; an eloquent design totally embracing the social, topographical, technical and financial aspects of its situation. It is interesting to compare the scale of our own opportunities and the quality of our resulting New Towns and speculative developments.

In our present time of social and technological change the designer's tasks become increasingly complex. The overlaps and interactions between the hardware and software of our time (cars, planes, television, communications, computers) and our building fabric make it increasingly difficult to conceive of architecture in terms of the traditional past.

The age-old definition of architecture as 'commodity, firmness and delight' is, however, still valid if the 'firmness' is realised by plastic and alloy instead of masonry, and the 'delight' is extended by current developments in electronic communications and climatic control.

The scope for new design solutions to meet both established and emerging needs is tremendous. It does not follow that we have to use untried techniques or ideas to innovate. Initiative taken on a prototype can determine vast potential on the open market. At one end of the scale new planning ideas allied with traditional techniques can often prove as significant as the utilisation of new materials and techniques in isolation. The real scope lies in the fusion of both, whatever the scale of assignment, from product design to city and regional planning, whether one-off projects or vast collective enterprises.

Design innovations which could change the appearance of buildings and make them more sensitive to our real needs can spring from a number of sources. These could be broadly classed under new techniques of planning, engineering and management. They can be separated out for examination in more detail, but in reality the design process itself would integrate these and other key factors.

First, new planning techniques. These are needed to satisfy today's rapidly changing social and technological patterns. Our spaces are becoming smaller but very highly mechanised. Like industrial plant it becomes uneconomic not to utilise them to the maximum effect. In planning terms this might mean spaces which have multi-purpose use. We also demand mobility and rapid change. Five-and-a-half million people in the United States are living in trailer homes, which are increasing at the rate of 300,000 a year.

Obsolescence, whether based on fashion or real change, will have radical implications. Our buildings will have to be planned for flexibility so that they can change, grow and adapt. As land becomes more precious we must reconcile these needs with buildings which are sensitive to areas of scenic beauty. There is no reason why our present squandering of natural resources, both visual and material wealth, should continue. Intensive coastal development for housing and industry, for example, could be achieved without extending our present 'suburbia-on-sea'.

Similarly, by abandoning out-of-date planning forms which are currently based on hangovers from the past, we could preserve the genuinely historic parts of our cities and revitalise them with a modern, 20th-century equivalent.

Second, new engineering techniques. Examples of these are new materials, structures, total energy concepts and the feedback of ideas from other sources such as the electronic and aerospace industries. At one extreme we have the large-scale potential. Vast areas can be enclosed with lightweight space-frame structures or inflatable plastic membranes. Full climatic control is feasible; the polar regions could be 'tropicalised' and desert areas cooled.

It is a sad reflection that it takes the stimulus of warfare to promote instant hospitals. A full surgical hospital unit, about our most complex building type, was dropped by helicopter on barren ground at Tay Ninh (Vietnam) quite recently. Complete with self-contained power-packs, its rubber-coated Dacron walls were inflated and the unit fully operational within a few hours.

Traditional site-based techniques are being replaced by factory-controlled components using new materials to achieve higher standards, speed and value for money. Some traditional materials like carpets are being completely reinterpreted by current technology. Mechanical equipment has become a major and fast-increasing proportion of the total building cost. Nevertheless, it is still in a very crude form (it is difficult to imagine anything more crude than our lavatories and waste-disposal systems), and we generally insert it into an already obsolete shell, complete with traditional plumbing. At the present time we are still in limbo; half embracing a craft-based past and half aware of a new engineering potential.

Thirdly, new techniques of management. Increasingly complex organisations involved with problem-posing (clients, communities) and problem-solving (designers, contractors, manufacturers) can no longer rely on intuitive judgements. Skilled programming and briefing techniques are becoming increasingly important. Cost and time factors should be welcomed as further performance disciplines. Cost-in-use will become an increasingly critical factor. Our cost planning, often based on first cost in isolation, is quite misleading.

Although the framework for teamwork exists, all too often designers act in isolation, leaving other specialists to 'make it work' in a passive role. The scope for really integrated teams with wide-ranging skills is considerable. Current divisions between design and production will be reduced, involving the designer in new and exciting roles closely allied to industry. It will be a paradox that as the organisations involved get larger, the scope for small groups to innovate will increase, either from within or outside the organisations. Although greater rationalisation will produce sophisticated components and kits-of-parts, there is every reason to suppose that, as in the field of business and politics, key individuals will still play a decisive role in the field of design.

In many ways, the design process is probably one of our cheapest commodities. It allows us the scope to explore many alternatives and possibilities before making any actual commitment in reality. All too often, however, it is the subject of short-cuts; an unnecessary fringe benefit to which lip service is occasionally paid, or a luxury for those prestige occasions. The results we suffer surround us and the loss at all levels is entirely our own.

(Article first published in BP Shield, *March 1969)*

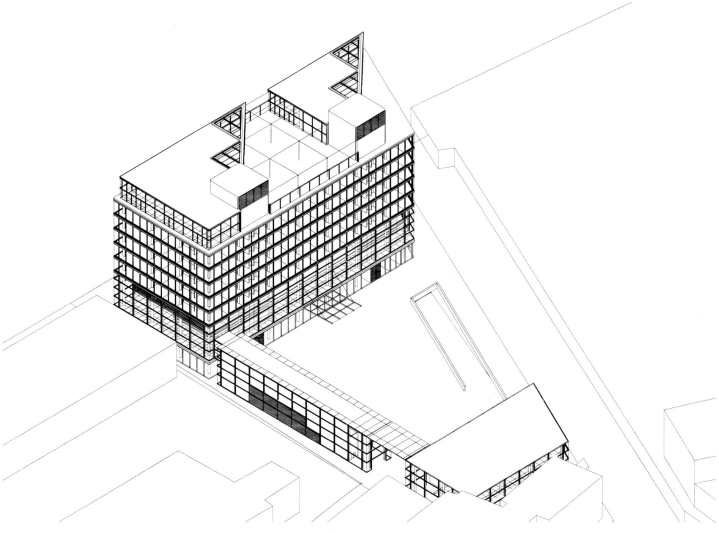

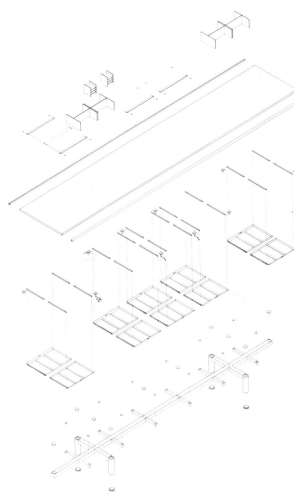

Riverside Offices & Apartments, Chelsea Reach, London

Foster Associates have recently moved from their two separate central London premises into a single new building of their own design on the South Bank of the Thames, between Albert Bridge and Battersea Bridge. The complex provides continuous riverside and dockside public walks including a bridge crossing the adjacent Ransomes Dock.

The project comprises a simple, elegant, eight-storey building along the river front, containing offices on the ground, first and mezzanine levels, 30 private apartments from levels three to seven and two studio penthouses. To the rear of the site is a two-storey glazed pavilion which will be used for offices.

The entrance to the development is under a glass canopy which links the pavilion with the Foster Associates office entrance. The top-lit exhibition space is eight metres high and 40m long, and provides a stepped route up to the first-floor reception on the river

front. A staff café overlooks the dramatic staircase. The main studio space is 60m long, 24m deep and 6.5m high, with a mezzanine along the south edge linking the service cores. At right angles to the north glass wall, 13 work benches, each 11m long, are arranged to allow everybody a river view. All services are contained under the raised floor with either floor outlets for air conditioning, or totems located under the benches for power, computer and telephone outlets.

Modelmaking, audio-visual presentation spaces and computer rooms are accommodated in the south 'service zone' above and below the mezzanine, with the library and all document filing located on banks of shelving on the core walls along the southern edge.

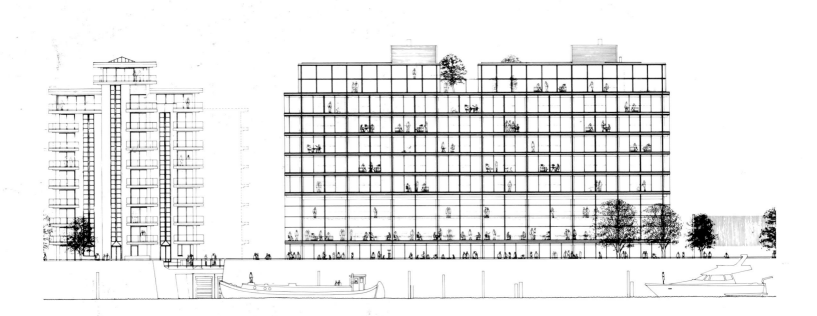

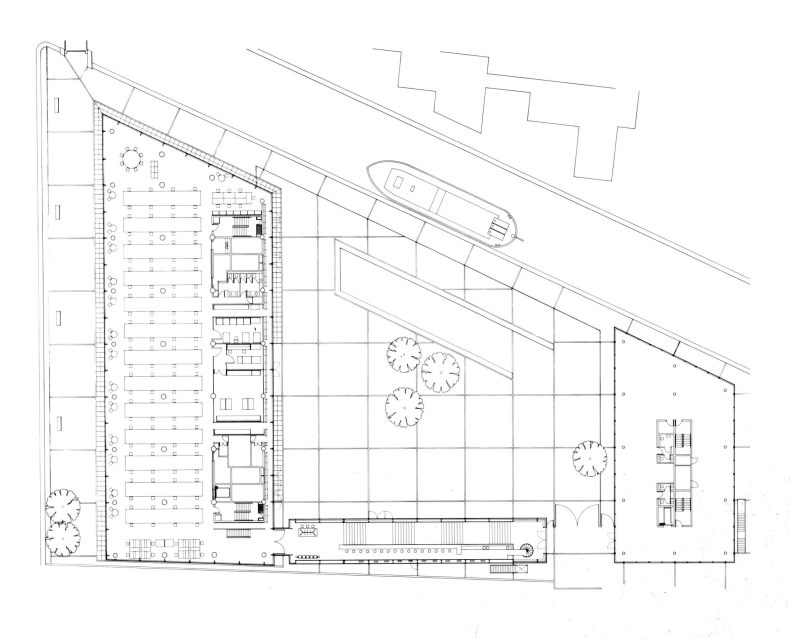

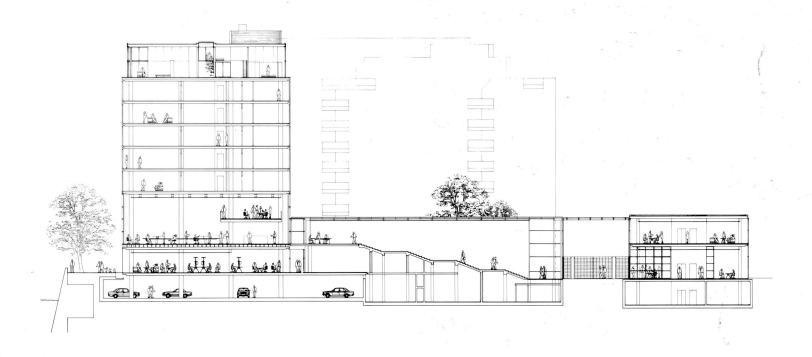

↖ Domestic departures ✈

↖ Domestic arrivals ✈

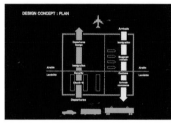

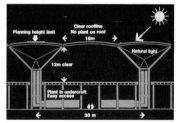

Third London Airport, Stansted

Foster Associates were first commissioned in 1981, but their brief grew steadily to encompass a British Rail station, stations for the tracked transit system, two satellites and ancillary buildings as well as the terminal itself and the masterplan for the terminal zone. This is important, because modern air journeys do not begin or end with terminals, even though the Stansted building is one of Foster Associates' most elegant and convincing structures.

The design stemmed from the general principle, warmly endorsed by the British Airport Authority's former chairman, Sir Norman Payne, that international air terminals had grown too complex for their own good; and that what was needed was a return to the pioneering days of civil aviation, when air travellers could proceed in a straight line from their parked cars to the aircraft, without going through all the infuriating changes of direction that disfigure most major airports. Accordingly at Stansted, despite the late

addition of a British Rail station the basic principle has been observed. From the set down point, the traveller moves in a straight line and at a constant level through the terminal building, from landside to airside or vice versa. In the process, travellers experience two architectural orders. The primary order is the lattice shelled roof structure, supported on the angled branches of 12m high structural trees; the smaller secondary order is the flexible system of freestanding enclosures such as shops, banks, kitchens and lavatories.

Of great importance at Stansted is the ceiling. The roof reverts to its primary purpose; to keep out the rain and let in the light. Rainwater is syphoned through horizontal channels to eight downpipes at each end of the building and natural light floods into the interior through triangular rooflights near the top of the roof domes.

The simplicity of the terminal interior is achieved by banishing services normally contained in the ceiling zone to an undercroft. This undercroft is the engine room of the building. It runs beneath the

entire area of the concourse and contains all the baggage handling and all the environmental engineering plant. The heating, ventilation, air conditioning and artificial light of the concourse are contained within the clusters of steel columns which rise up through the floor – the 'trunks' of the structural trees.

At Stansted, the transition from landside to airside is marked symbolically by a change from stone to wool. On the landside, grey granite slabs; on airside a specially woven carpet, its simple grid pattern of warm greys matching the flecks in the polished stone.

From the terminal, a Tracked Transit System (TTS) leads to the first two satellite buildings designed to handle the expected eight million passengers a year. The satellite is a narrow finger of a building which adjoins the aircraft parking stands. It is quite a complex building in its own right as it has to provide a TTS link, arrival and departure levels and a concourse for gate lounges. The upper level concourse has a grandstand view of the apron

through fully glazed external walls and it provides the first and last views of the terminal before air travellers move down a level and walk through the link bridges onto the aircraft.

Stansted is in the tradition of a newer energy-conscious series of buildings by Foster Associates. By digging the bulk of the building into the contours of the site, its roofline drops below the treeline – an important issue in the environmental debate and at the public inquiries which finally allowed the project to proceed.

***Above left**: Atlanta Airport in 1925: primitive, but very direct in its relationship between passengers and aircraft.*

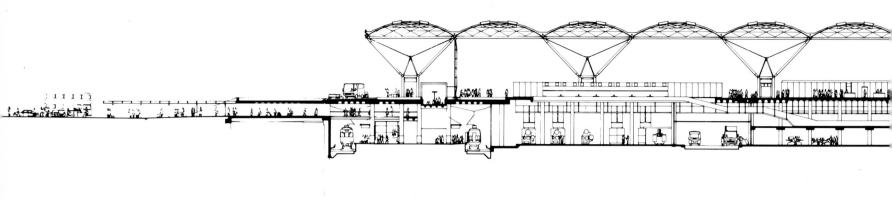

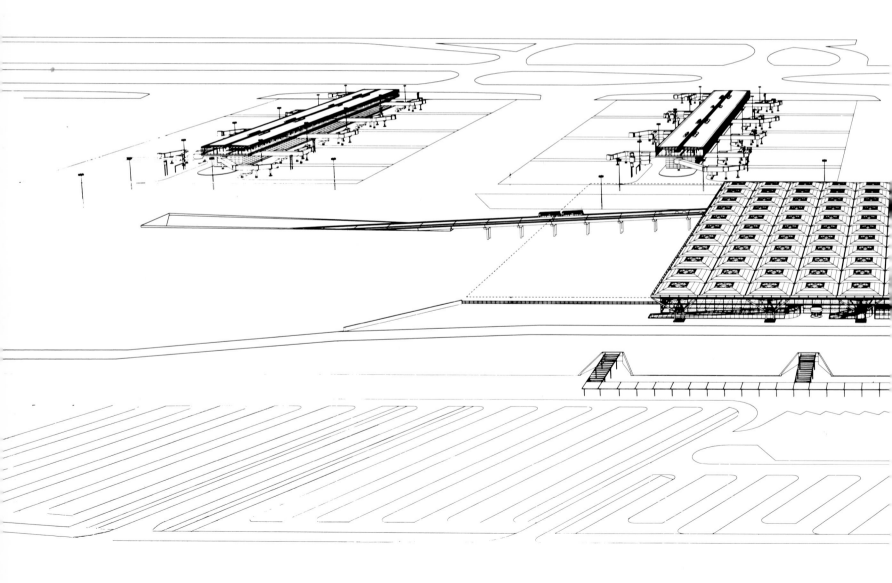

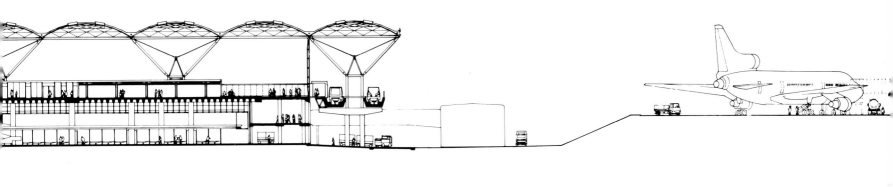

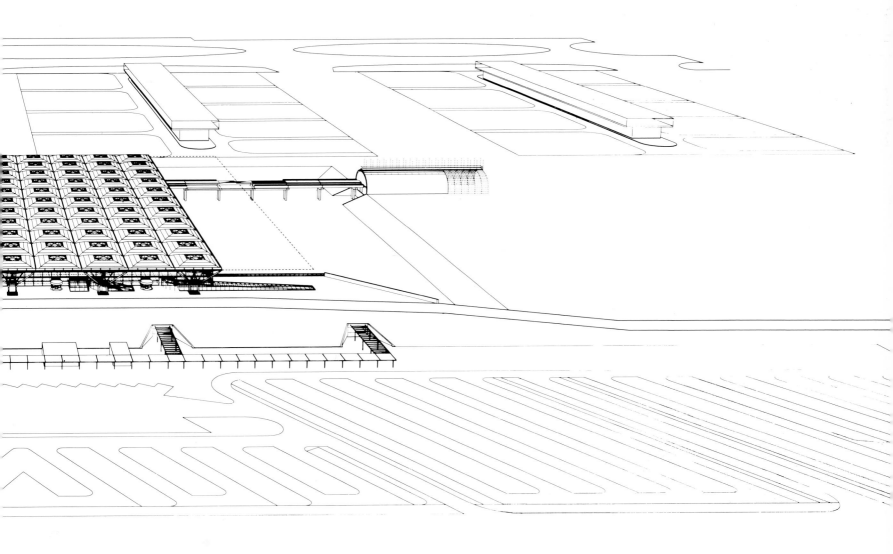

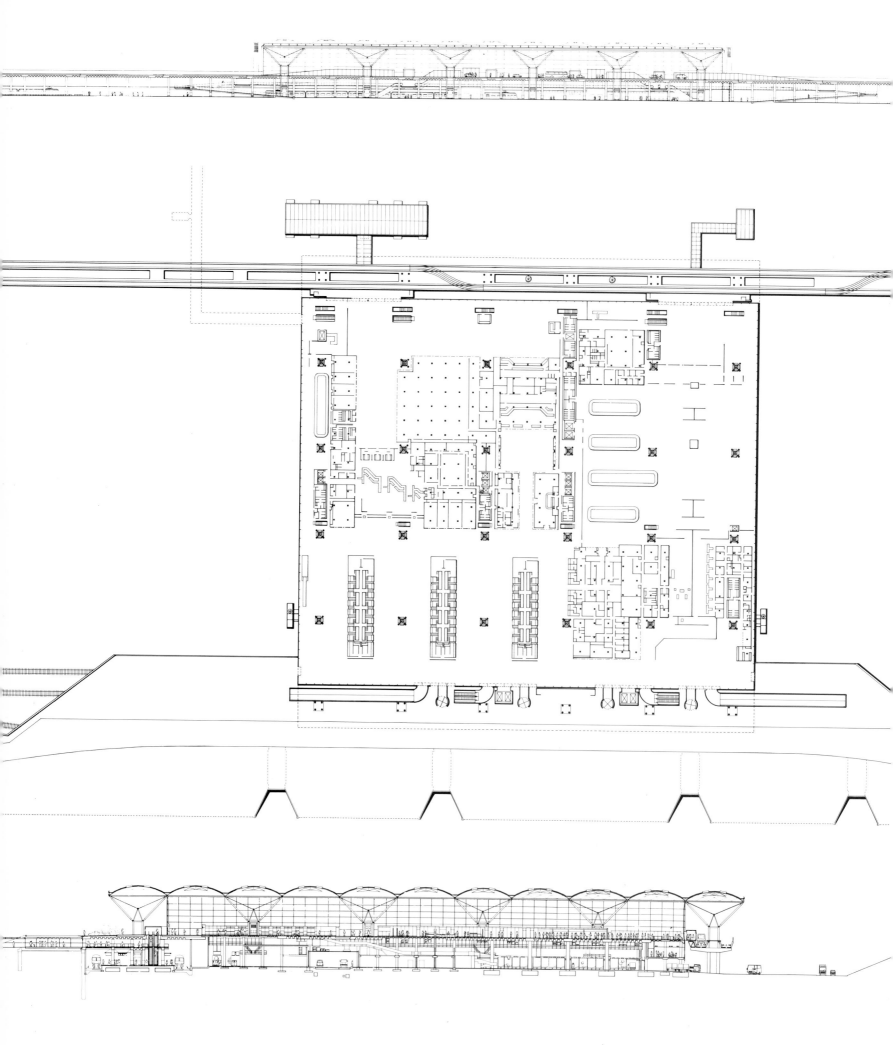

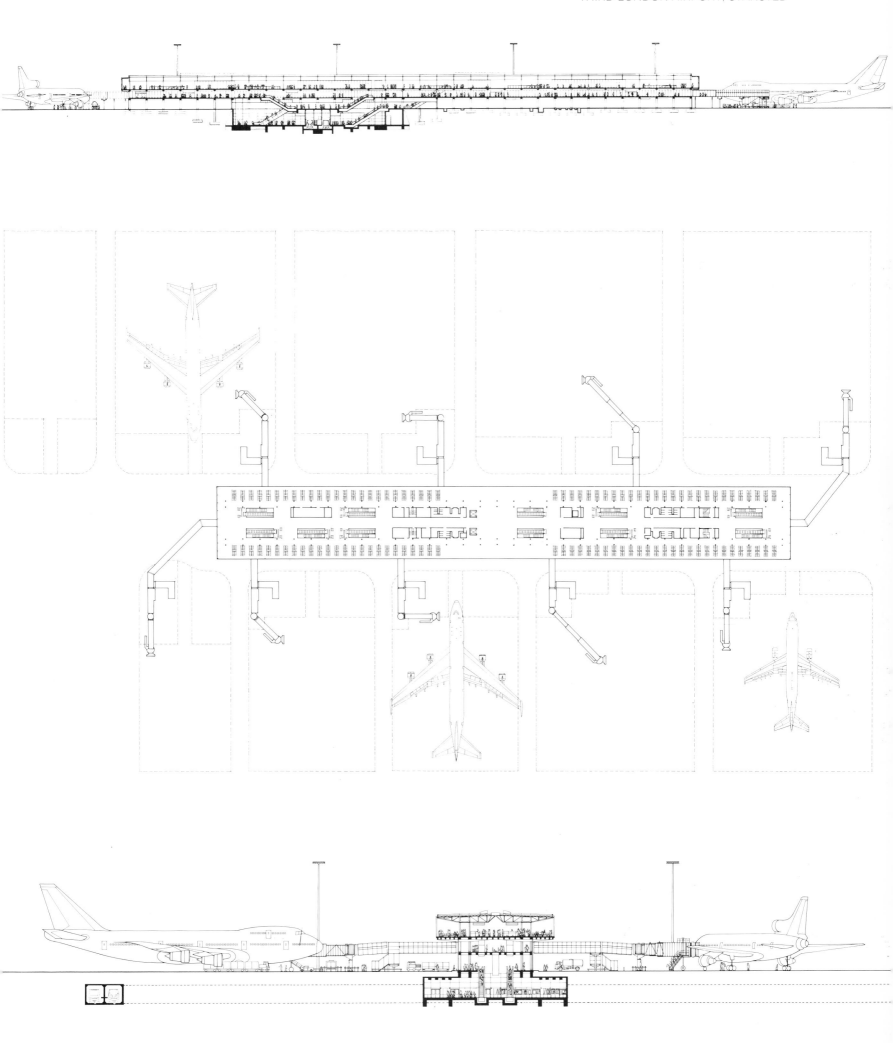

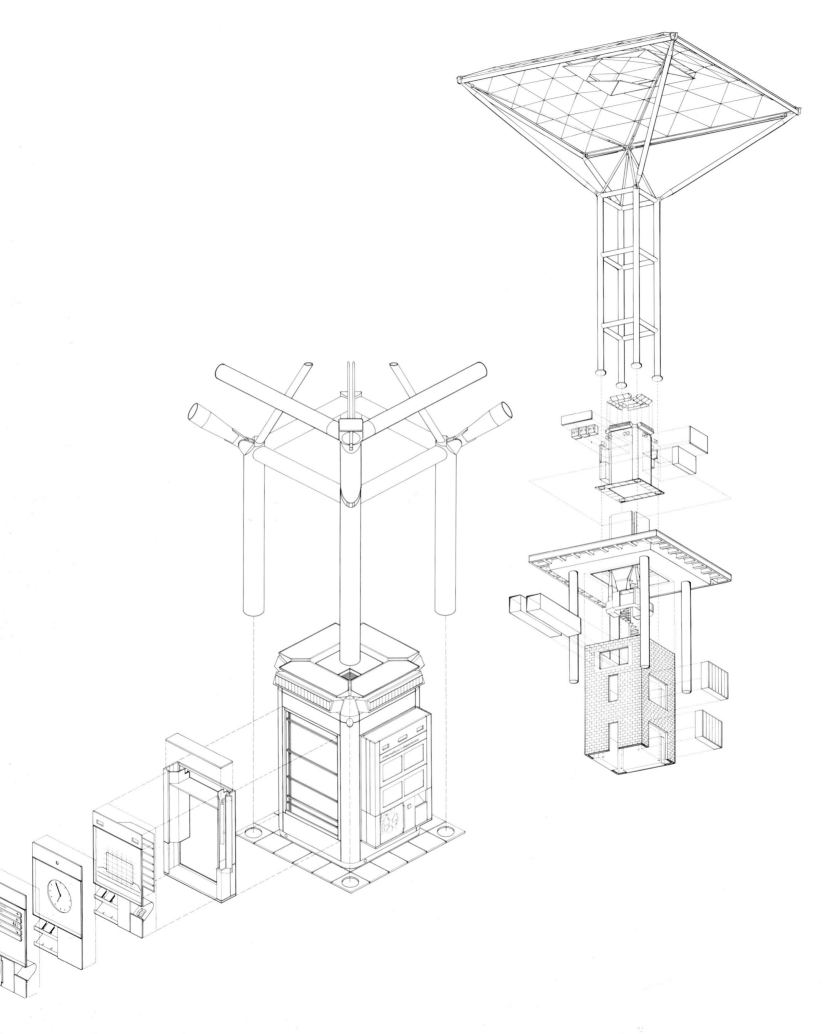

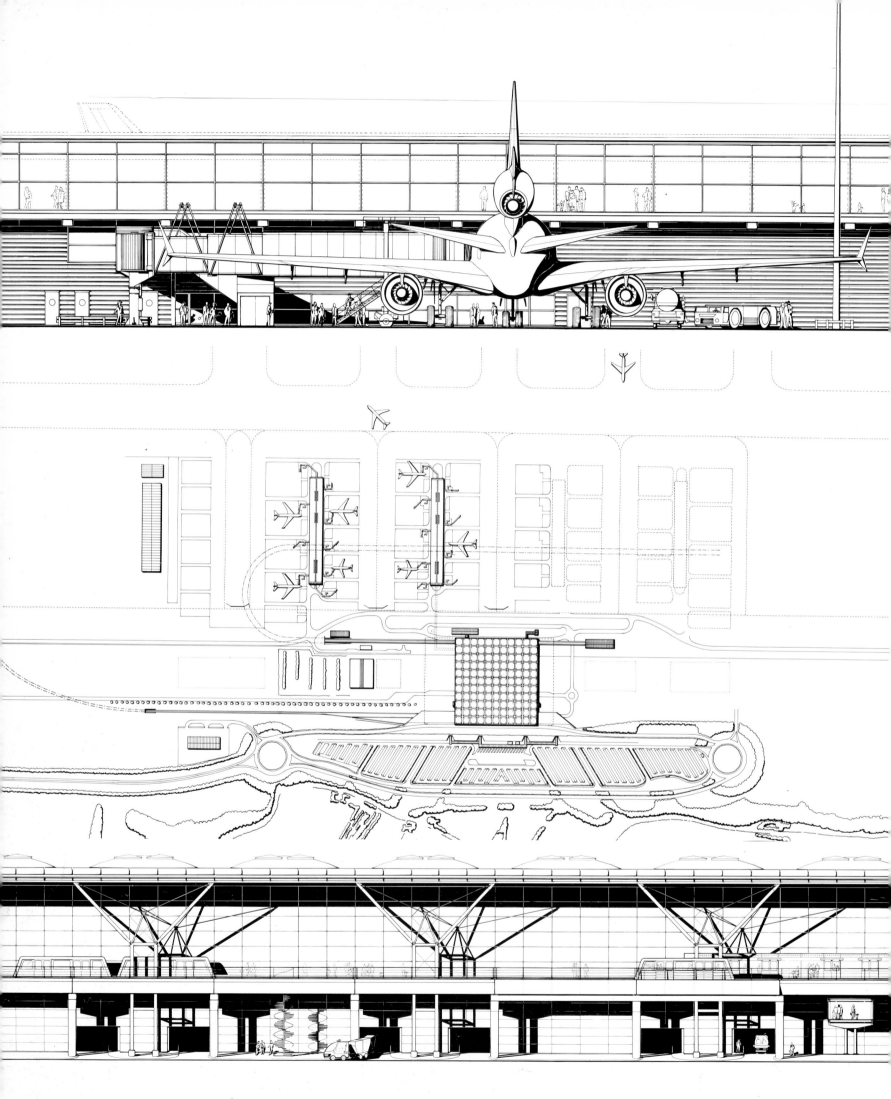

46

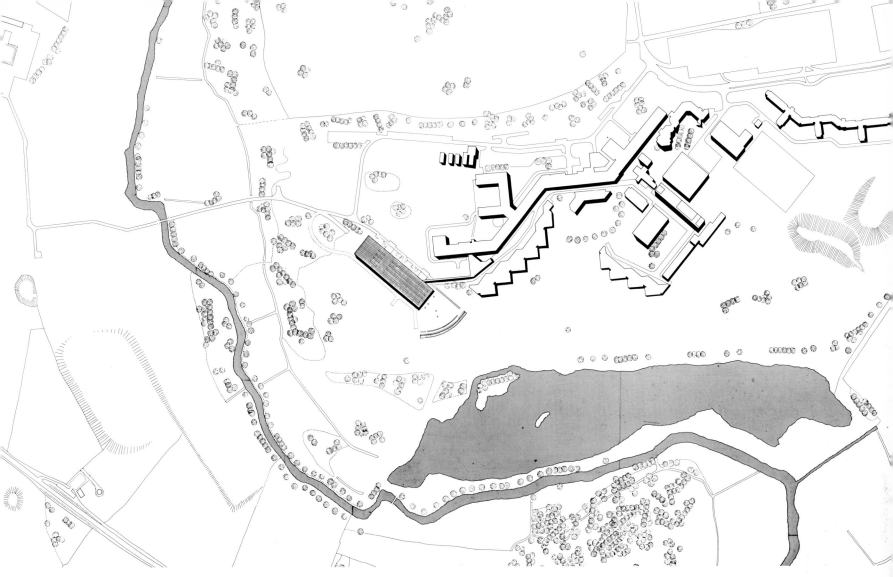

Crescent Wing, Sainsbury Centre for the Visual Arts, Norwich

The Crescent Wing is the result of a major new benefaction by the Centre's founders, Sir Robert and Lady Sainsbury, providing vital space to show the reserve collection as well as accommodation for conferences and temporary exhibitions and conservation workshops.

The decision to extend the Centre provided a dilemma for architects and clients. The building is an open-ended structure implying linear growth. Why should the basic container not be extended? The Sainsburys, however, saw the Centre as a finite object, perfect in itself. The only course was therefore to extend the building underground.

Much of the Centre is below ground: a basement given over to services, storage and vehicle access. It made sense to extend the basement, particularly since the ground fell away in front of the building, towards the lake. The

extended basement could therefore naturally emerge into the open air and have a glazed frontage to the lake.

Foster broke with the rectilinear geometry of the original building to create a fan-shaped extension, in its parkland setting. There had to be a conjunction between the two buildings, however – achieved by putting the offices in a radial arc facing out with the gallery behind, in a fan shaped space. Study collections and workshops fit well into the remaining rectangle.

Outside, a grass lawn, perforated by 1.8m sq glass rooflights, hints that there may be something underneath, but only when you look back at the Centre from the lake does the new building reveal itself, with a great sweep of inclined planes of fritted glass.

Foster has grappled here with a problem which affects many great architects: how to extend and adapt their own works. Opening in a year which saw another Foster building (Willis Faber at Ipswich) listed Grade I, it shows that he is not content merely to embalm his own inventions.

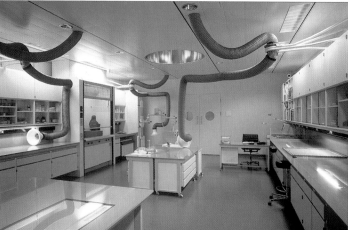

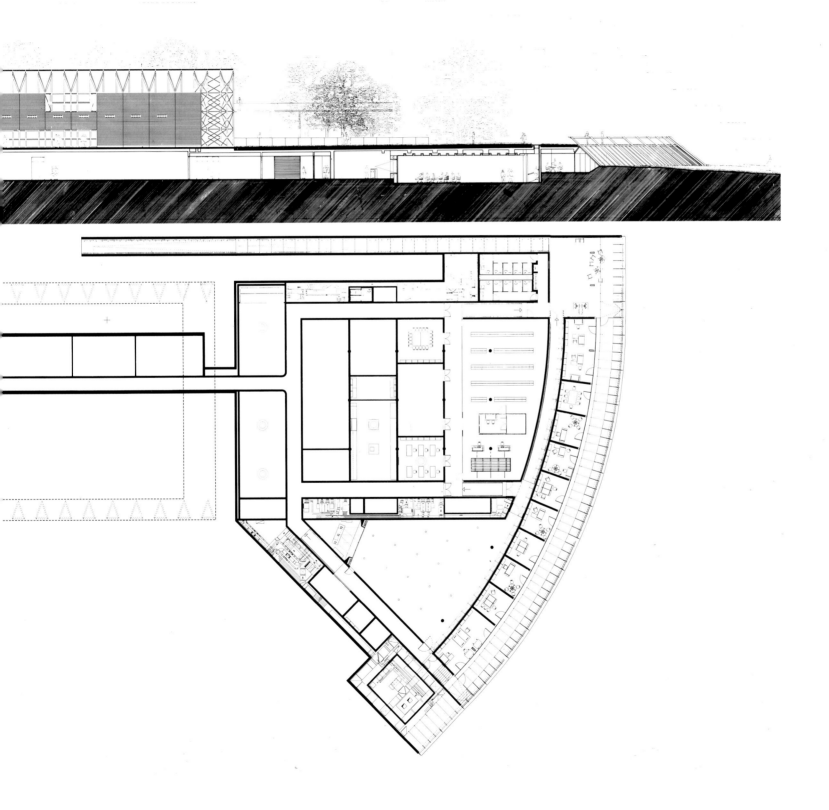

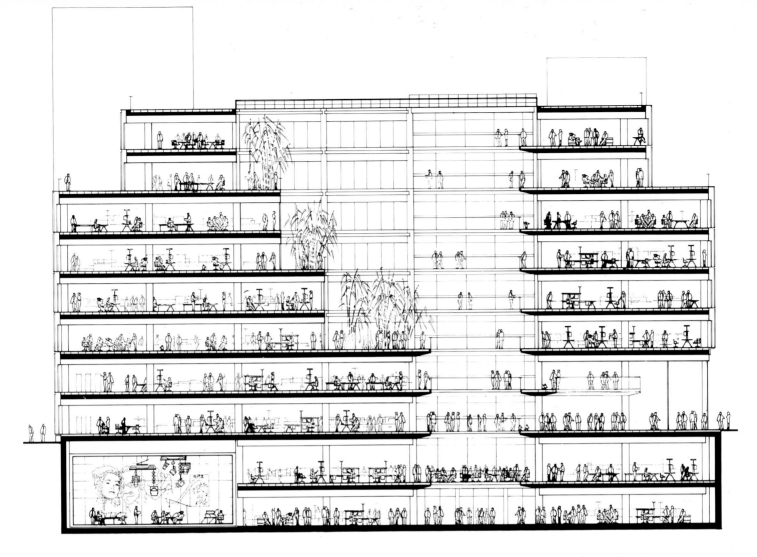

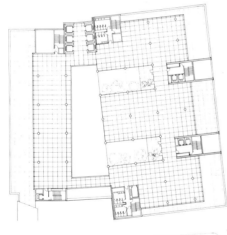

ITN Headquarters, London

The ITN site was previously a newspaper printing plant. Its deep basement, once occupied by printing presses, is now open to a vast atrium surrounded by news rooms, television studios and dozens of high-technology editing suites. This dramatic space passes through every floor of the building and is the focus for all internal activities. High-speed glass lifts link the different levels to a series of balconies and internal terraces, lit from all sides and from above by a mixture of clear and translucent glass.

The all-round openness is achieved by an innovative clear glass envelope, consisting of an inner and outer wall. Air is passed in the space between these two layers and forms part of the energy-efficient system that heats and cools the entire building.

The mass of the building is reduced at street level with large setbacks on all elevations. These were designed after a close dialogue with the planners at Camden and maintain the existing urban scale and streetscape.

To achieve an on-air date by the end of 1990, the development, a joint venture between ITN and Stuart Lipton's Stanhope Properties, was built to a record-tight programme. The first concrete for the new building was poured in June 1989. Barely 18 months later in December 1990, ITN made their first broadcast from the building, which was completed on time and within a commercial developer's budget.

55

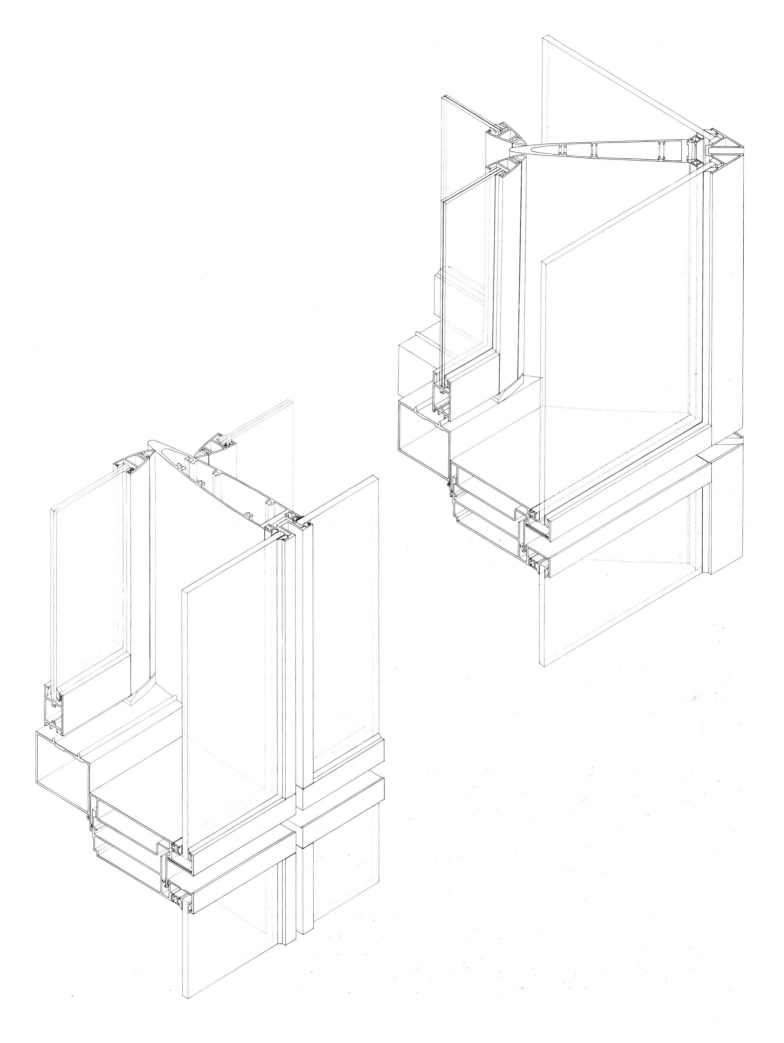

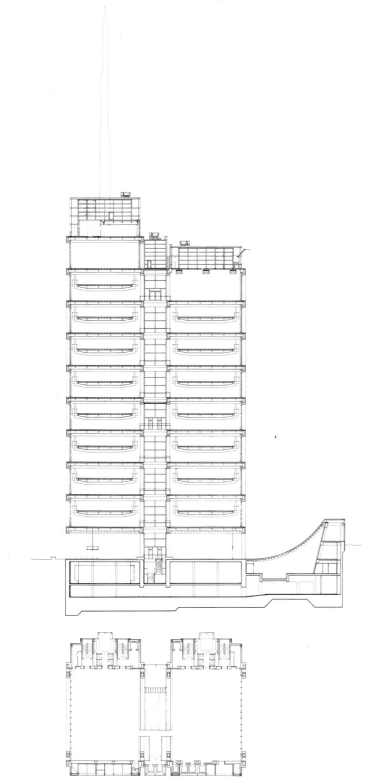

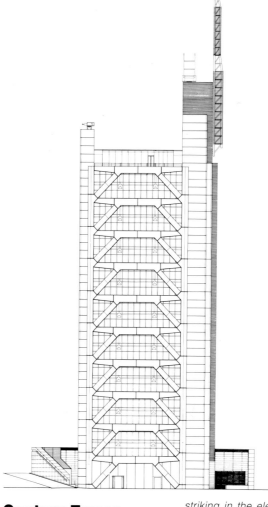

Century Tower, Tokyo

Century Tower, which opened on 27 May 1991, is Foster Associates' first contribution to the ever-changing skyline of Tokyo, and the first completed Foster project in Japan, where it set a new standard for speculative office development. The building inevitably evokes memories of past Foster projects such as the spectacular Hongkong Bank, but equally represents a specific response to the very different physical and cultural context of Japan.

Designed jointly by Foster Associates' London and Tokyo offices for the Obunsha Publishing Group, Century Tower consists of two linked towers, 19 and 21 storeys high respectively, separated by a full-height atrium which brings light into the very heart of the building and is expressed on the side elevations. The office floors are arranged in dramatic double-height units – bridged, in effect, between the service cores at either side of each tower. The braced frame is as visually

striking in the elevations as it is structurally expressive, and has the practical benefits of keeping the office space free of columns and other interruptions.

Norman Foster is celebrated for his concern with natural light, but in this instance Foster Associates responded in particular to the luminosity of traditional Japanese interiors. Daylight pours into the atrium, which is fully open to the office floors on either side. This arrangement involved an innovative approach to fire and smoke control. At ground level, the entrance lobby is again naturally lit – an essentially public meeting place.

Century Tower is the outcome of an exceptionally happy collaboration with the Japanese construction industry and with an international group of consultants and sub-contractors. It meets the needs of late 20th-century business with a design which in its energy, grace and integrity combines lasting Eastern and Western values.

Sackler Galleries, Royal Academy of Arts, London

The Sackler Galleries represent a radical remodelling of the Victorian Diploma Galleries, which were relatively little used because of their inadequate servicing and poor access. The new galleries, created in the shell of the old, naturally lit from above, with a sophisticated system of louvres to monitor light levels, are fully air conditioned and thus suitable for prestigious loan exhibitions.

The problem of access has been solved by inserting both a new staircase and a glass-walled lift in the lightwell between the original Burlington House and the Victorian galleries behind. In the process, the facade of Burlington House has been revealed after more than a century hidden from view. The new lift and staircase provide easy communication between all floors of the Academy, while remaining completely invisible from the entrance hall and main staircase. The scheme provides a new system of circulation around the complex building

to cope with its ever increasing number of visitors, and access for disabled and infirm visitors is now vastly improved.

A striking feature of the scheme is the new reception area, sitting over the original lightwells and incorporating the parapet of the main galleries as a plinth for sculpture. Glazed edges allow daylight to penetrate the space below. It also includes a permanent, secure location for the Academy's most precious possession, the Michelangelo Tondo.

The project demonstrates the practice's careful evaluation of what exists and strategy for beneficial change. Long-neglected areas of the building will form the new axis for visitors, and the rich history of the building has been revealed in the process.

Above: The present frontage of the Royal Academy: an elaborate Victorian gloss on a Georgian town house.
Centre: The original Burlington House was one of London's grandest residences. **Below**: The 'gap' between Burlington House and the large galleries added by the Victorians was a forgotten void, invisible to visitors and without function.

67

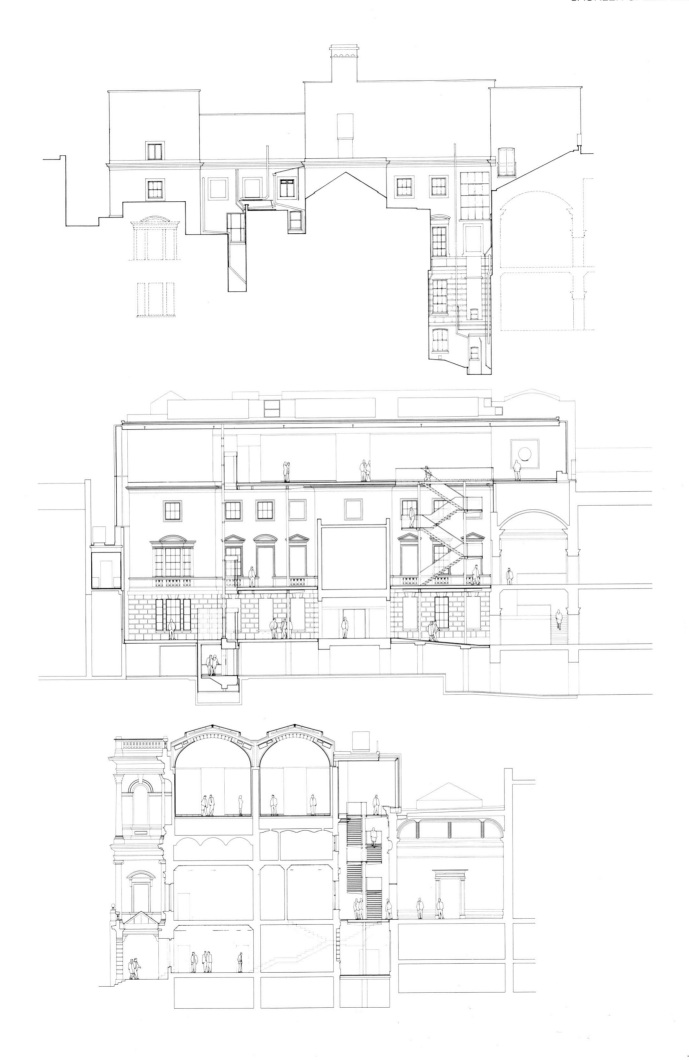

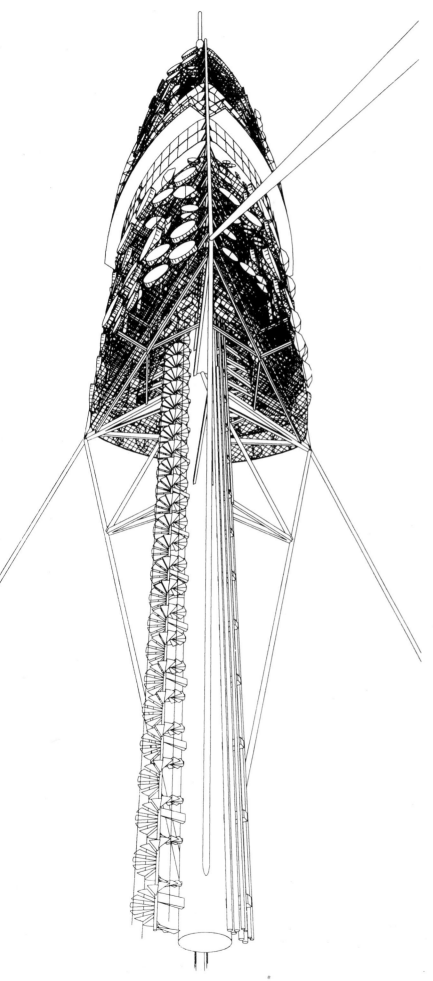

Telecommunications Tower, Barcelona

Foster's designs for the Barcelona Telecommunications Tower were successful in a limited international competition in July 1988. (The City was adamant that a rash of new towers would not be permitted and insisted on a competition.)

The structure, which will be completed in time for the Olympic Games in Barcelona, the World Cup in Madrid and Expo 92 in Seville, will occupy a commanding position on a mountain top above the city. The design of the tower follows the Foster philosophy of achieving maximum effect with minimal structural means. The starting point is a narrow-diameter shaft of precast concrete components which rests on a single foundation pad. This core is braced by three vertical steel trusses set at 120 degrees to one another, and the whole structure is tethered to post-tensioned guys anchored in the mountain side. The modular floors and platforms are suspended from this structural skeleton and have been designed for flexibility and future change.

The plan form – an equilateral triangle with curved sides – has been designed to offer minimum wind resistance and maximum resistance to drift, twist and vibration. Considerable attention has been paid to safety and maintenance. Lift shafts, stairs and cable risers are grouped on the outside of the shaft for ease of access, and the high-strength tension guys have been designed in such a way that up to one third of their constituent cables can be removed for inspection or replacement without impairing the stability of the tower. Each of the three rock anchors will have a triple corrosion protection system. This will consist of a polyester resin jacket for the anchor, surrounded by a polypropylene sleeve which in turn will be embedded in cement. As a precaution against sabotage all three primary guys will be protected top and bottom with resilient bomb sleeves backed up by close-circuit television monitoring and movement detectors.

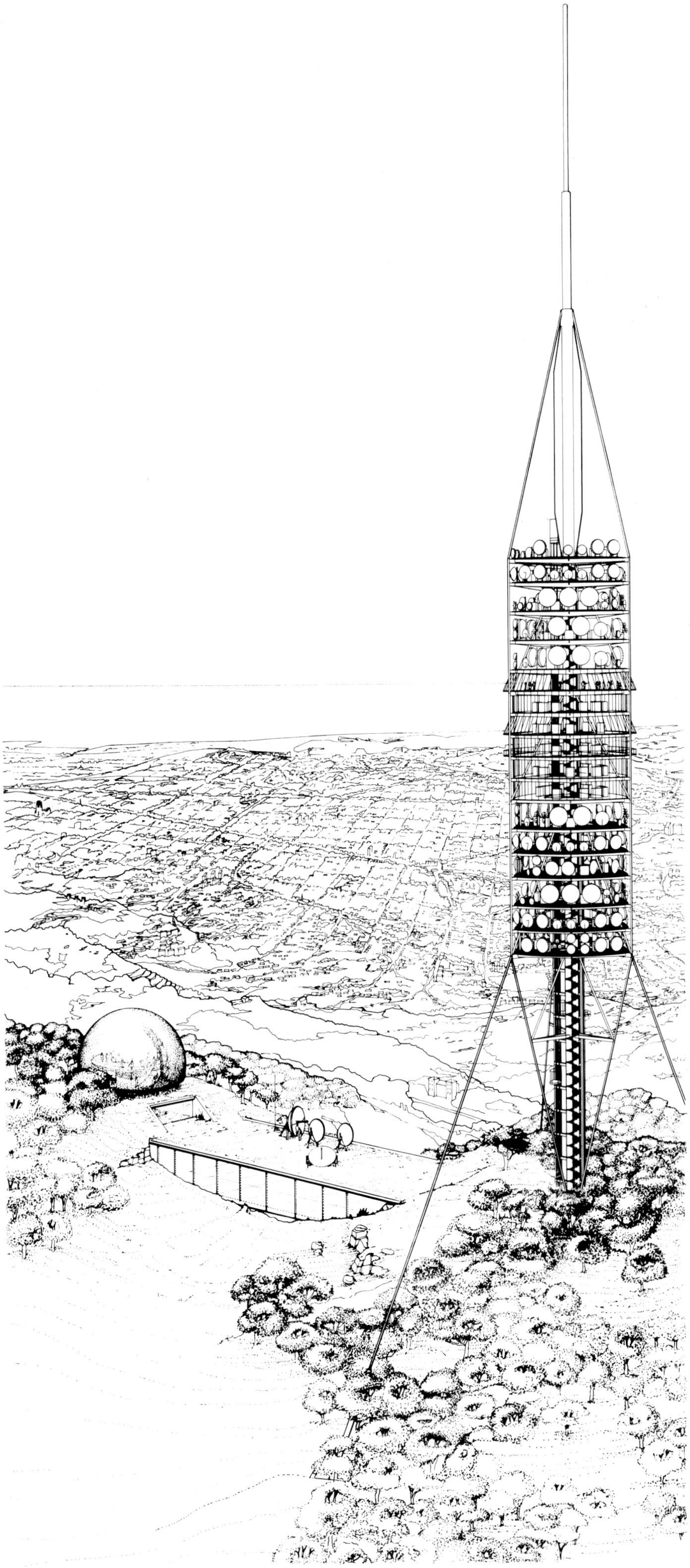

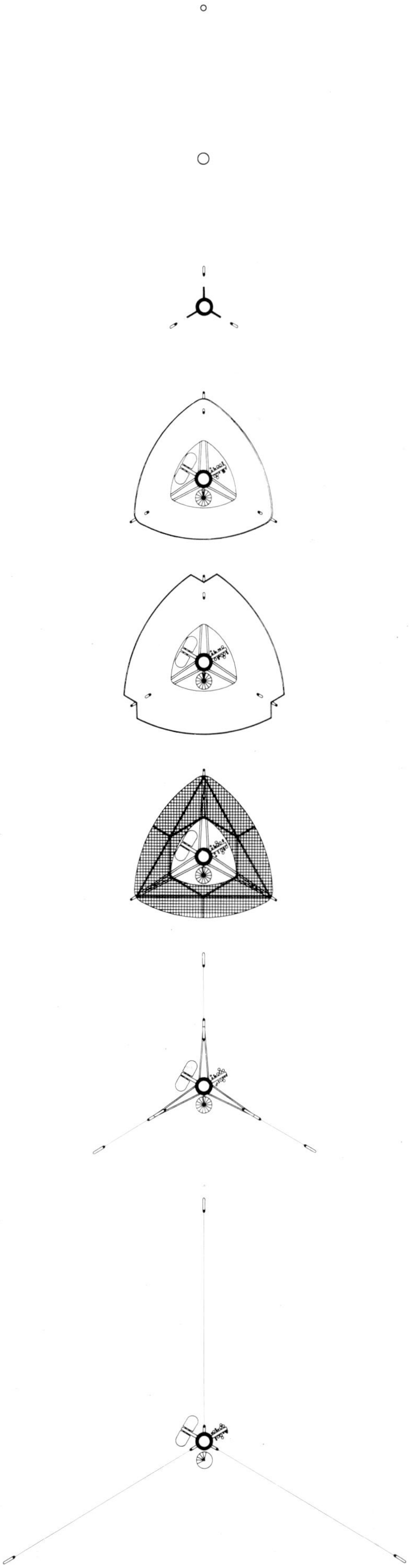

Carré d'Art, Nîmes

The Carré d'Art (or Médiathèque) in the ancient city of Nîmes is certain to be a landmark in the continuing development of Foster's work during the 1990s – though the original commission dates from 1984. In that year Foster Associates won an international competition, beating Gehry, Pelli and Nouvel. The project demanded a sensitive response to the site, just yards from one of the finest surviving Roman buildings, the Maison Carrée, and to the climate of Nîmes (where summers can be scorchingly hot). Foster's approach – disciplined but contemporary – seems entirely appropriate for the location. Planned to a strict grid, the new arts centre is raised up on a plinth of local stone – a 'Classical' device which helps to set it firmly in the street as well as providing practical protection against occasional flooding.

The Carré d'Art – due to open in 1992 and widely dubbed the 'Pompidou of the South' – is a relatively large building, yet it succeeds in looking quite modest.

It replaces a 19th-century theatre, burned out some years ago and subsequently abandoned, and the designs provide for a new building roughly equivalent in scale to its predecessor. To achieve this, a considerable amount of accommodation – including the cinema and auditorium as well as services and storage – has been placed below ground level. The galleries are located on top of the building, together with a café/bar, with the library below. The centrepiece is the dramatic five-storey internal courtyard, which pays regard to a regional tradition. Beyond this, the designs are strongly influenced by both Japanese architecture and by Chareau's Maison de Verre.

Indeed, Nîmes is the location for Foster's supreme act of reverence to that great Parisian monument. The protracted construction period has allowed the design team to develop the concept of the glazing scheme, which includes clear, opaque and 'fritted' panels, into a veritable broad palette of glass. The glass stair, recalling that in London's Royal Academy Sackler Galleries, is wide and monumental,

providing for a large number of visitors. It is accompanied by glazed hydraulic lifts.

The scheme has gone through a number of fascinating variations since its initial conception. The present version is the most refined, and the most uncompromising. Instructively, it is also the most appropriate for the site. Here, as in the Sackler Galleries, Foster dares to oppose minimal detailing and fine modern materials – some of the glass has only recently been patented – against a setting which could not be more historic or 'traditional'. In both cases, the gamble succeeds triumphantly. The Carré d'Art will be one of the key European buildings of the 90s.

__Opposite above__: The previous context of the Maison Carrée included the portico of the 19th-century theatre. Foster's new building responds to the Classical monument with an equal – if very different – rigour. __Above left__: The internal courtyard of the building echoes the courts and yards found in the ancient heart of Nîmes.

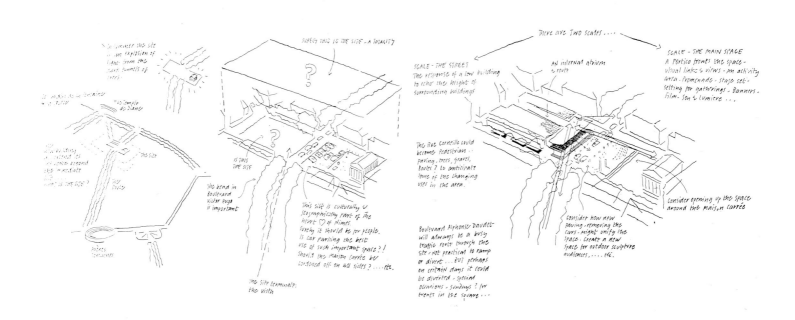

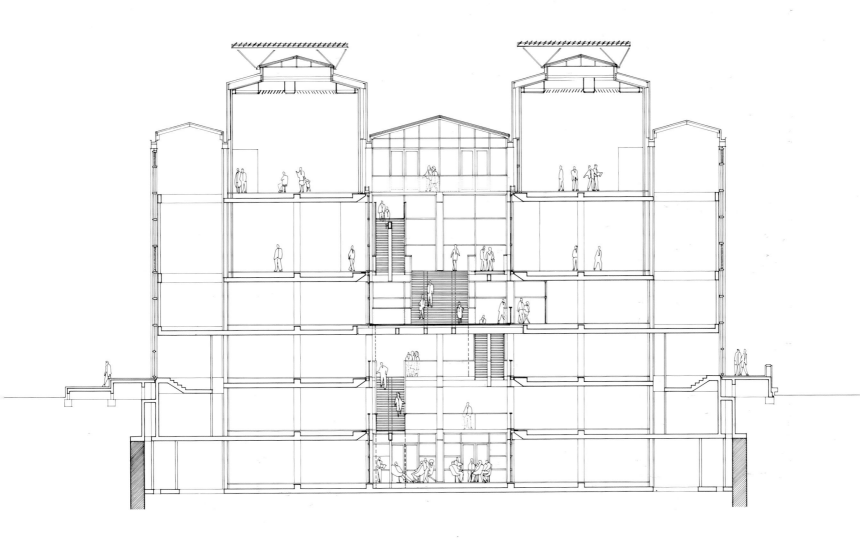

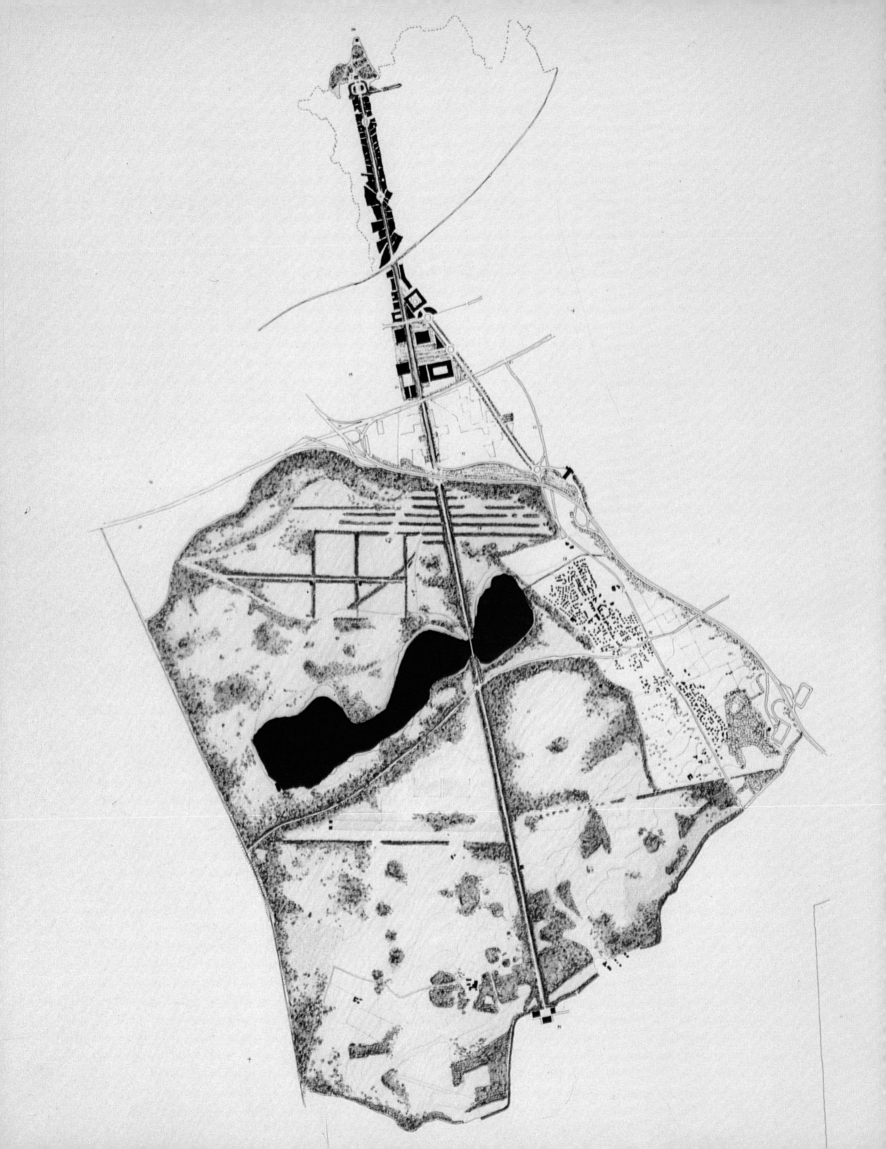

Masterplan, Avenue Jean Jaurès, Nîmes

The city of Nîmes like many in the south of France is entering a period of transition and change. This historic centre is under pressure to allow development yet still preserve the essential character that makes the city so attractive. The development of other locations around the city have taken place usually independently of any overall strategic masterplan.

With this as a background Nîmes established the Agency of Urbanism with the specific task of introducing planning guidelines and control methods that will allow Nîmes to expand. As a pilot project the Avenue Jean Jaurès and its extension to the motorway was selected. This route passes through many diverse areas with their own problems and complexities, and is very representative of the issues that affect the whole of this southern expansion zone. Foster Associates were commissioned to work closely with the agency to develop masterplan proposals for this route.

In working sessions with the agency, existing proposals under consideration for the southern area were examined. During these meetings the concept of extending Avenue Jean Jaurès to link with a new and large scale proposed development close to the airport gradually emerged.

This axis created new possibilities, a focus for important development areas closer to the city, and a new connection directly to the airport. A large part of this route is through open countryside, and a central concern is to establish a strong, clearly defined green belt where no development can take place.

The new route has the potential to act as a generator for new public amenities in the form of open space, parkland, sports etc, and other forms of recreation. The opportunity to integrate the agricultural nature of this area which must also be preserved, with new proposals will generate a unique concept for public open space particular to Nîmes.

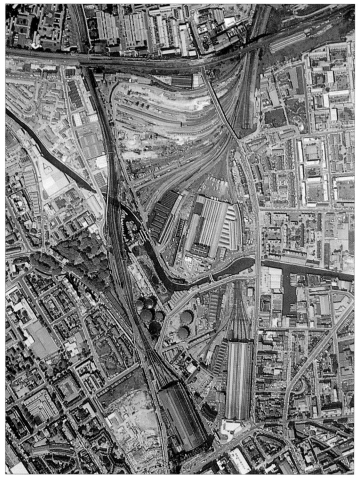

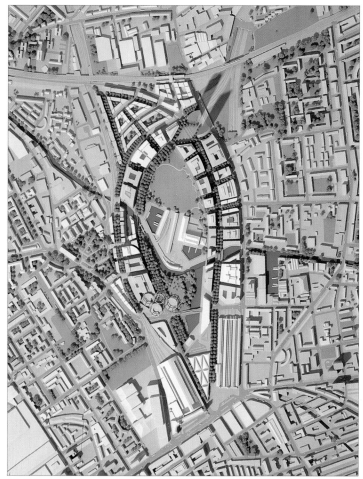

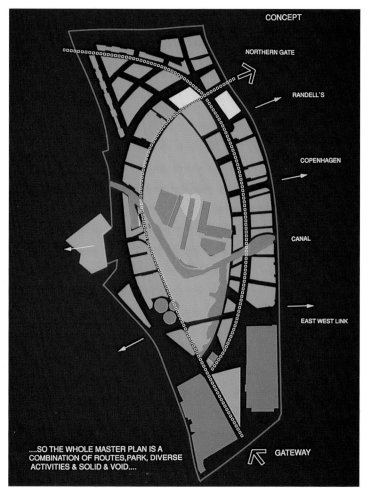

CONCEPT

NORTHERN GATE

RANDELL'S

COPENHAGEN

CANAL

EAST WEST LINK

....SO THE WHOLE MASTER PLAN IS A
COMBINATION OF ROUTES, PARK, DIVERSE
ACTIVITIES & SOLID & VOID....

GATEWAY

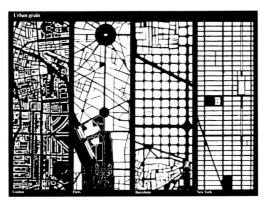

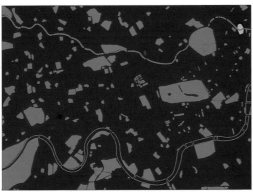

King's Cross Masterplan, London

The redevelopment of the King's Cross site – the railway land lying between King's Cross and St Pancras stations and bisected by the Regent's Canal – is one of the greatest opportunities in Europe for decisive inner-city renewal.

Invited to propose a masterplan for this massive 125-acre site, Foster Associates have identified three main elements: the great train sheds of King's Cross and St Pancras, with their glazed vaulted roofs; the Grand Union/Regent's Canal, which runs east to west through the site; and a number of important listed buildings and structures connected with railway history.

The plan consists of three main elements. At the Euston Road end a glazed vault wedged between the train sheds of King's Cross and St Pancras forms a majestic entrance canopy. It will shield a vast transport interchange for the two mainline railway termini and the Underground system, as well as providing a future starting point for British Rail's new rail link to Stansted airport, and a link with the Channel Tunnel.

Beyond this lies an elliptical six-acre park surrounded by commercial developments the scale and density of which have yet to be decided. Both entrance vault and park would be linked by a glazed shopping arcade. These are the three main elements, but many variations are possible. The purpose of the scheme is to stimulate critical reaction and public debate.

Opposite left centre: *An aerial picture shows the traditional industrial landscape, complete with monumental gasholders.* ***Opposite left below***: *The historic canal survives – and will be protected.* ***Opposite right below***: *Foster's scheme centres on a new urban park and great crescents of buildings.* ***Left above***: *The urban grain of London – contrasted with that of Paris, New York and Barcelona.* ***Left centre***: *King's Cross will give London a new green space.* ***Left below***: *The new street pattern will continue that of existing streets, breaking down the artificial barrier of the old goods yard.*

King's Cross Terminal, London

The proposed new terminal at King's Cross closes the southern end of the 52-acre redevelopment site. The original proposal was for a single arch span linking – and complementing – the famous Victorian train sheds of St Pancras and King's Cross; the present version is conceived as a free-standing structure which addresses sensitive heritage issues by its smaller scale and physical separation from the stations on either side. The structure is wedge shaped on plan (90mx180m) and based on structural concrete shells springing from columns at 30m centres. All columns, with the exception of one central column, are positioned at the perimeter, and curved glazing panels between the concrete shells admit daylight into the terminal space. There are direct connections at deck level with St Pancras and King's Cross stations and as at Stansted all services have been kept below the level of the main concourse.

Left above: *King's Cross station was a handsome piece of urban architecture – until encumbered with later additions.*
Left centre: *St Pancras station: one of the finest products of the railway age.*
Left below: *The railways were associated with rapid industrialisation which produced overcrowded cities and slums.*

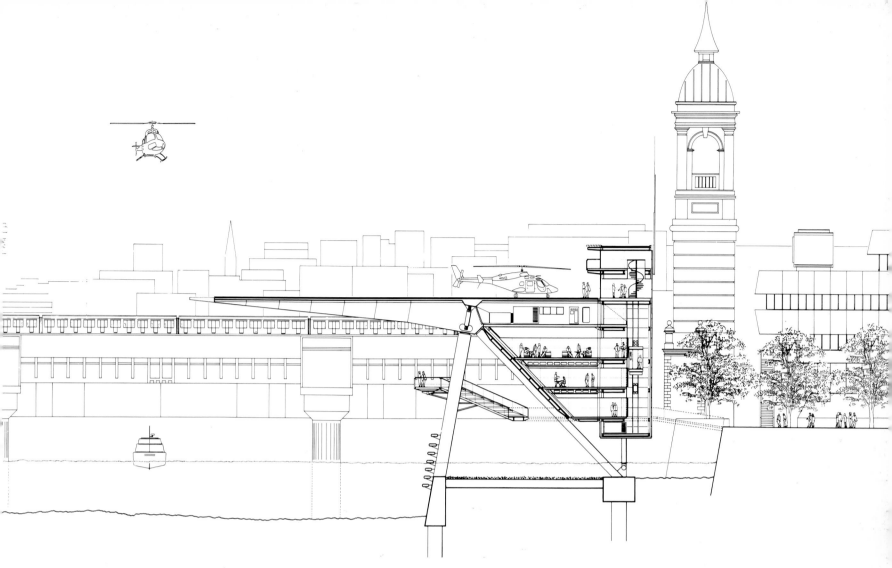

Heliport,
City of London

The need for a heliport in the City of London has long been recognised and discussed. Heliports in central London existed briefly in the 1980s, but today the nearest is at Battersea, which is not only too far away but incapable of expanding to meet demand. The site selected for the proposed City Heliport is on the river next to Cannon Street station and well within walking distance of all City offices. The main factors governing its design are environmental impact (especially noise) and safety. Positioning the heliport on the river and next to a noisy mainline station provided not only the safest location but also one where the impact of air traffic movement would be kept to a minimum. The cantilevered deck is 48m sq and 20m above the water; it is intended as a late-20th-century counterpart to Cannon Street railway bridge. The design includes viewing terraces, operational offices and a link to the riverside walkway.

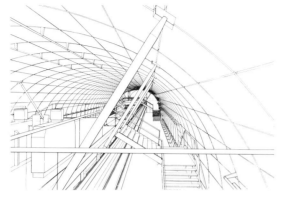

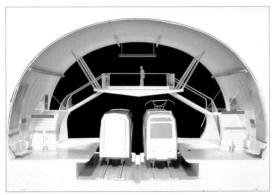

Metro Railway System, Bilbao

In 1988 the Department of Transportation and Public Works of the Basque Government held a limited competition for the design of Bilbao's metropolitan railway system. They were looking for an exciting design to redeem the poor architectural quality of public service building in the Basque region of Spain and, through a limited international competition, selected the Foster proposals as the clearest and most elegant solution. The essence of the scheme is the 16m-wide station cavern constructed in steel-shuttered concrete and carefully lit to reveal construction lines. Subsidiary to this is a minor order of prefabricated elements – mezzanines, ticket barriers, stairs, lifts etc, designed to provide contrast with the scale and solidity of the caverns. At street level the Metro is announced by hooded glass enclosures which admit daylight to the access tunnels and, at night, glow from within.

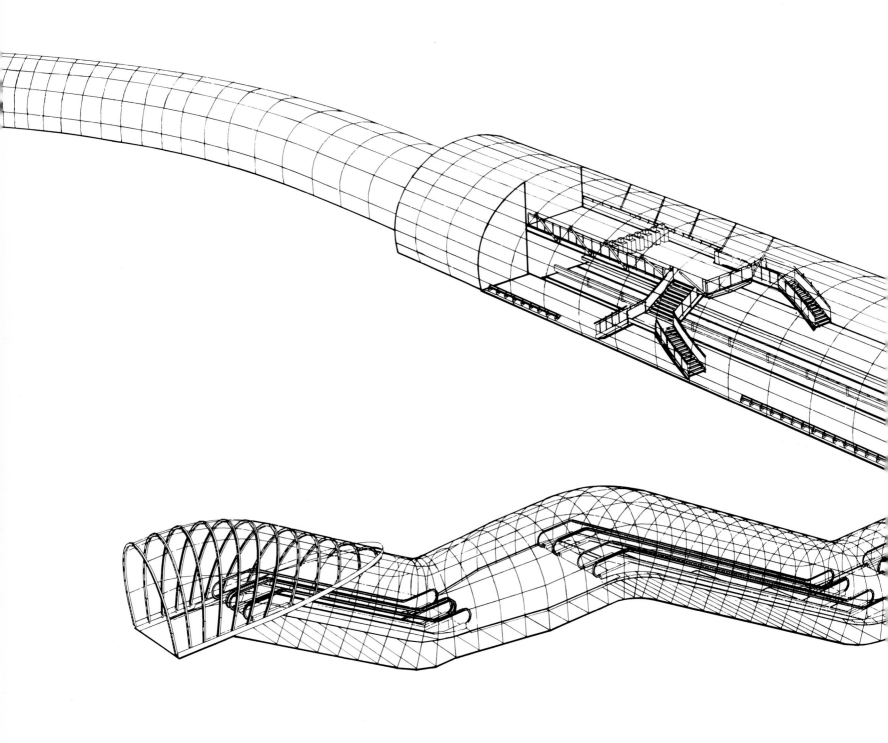

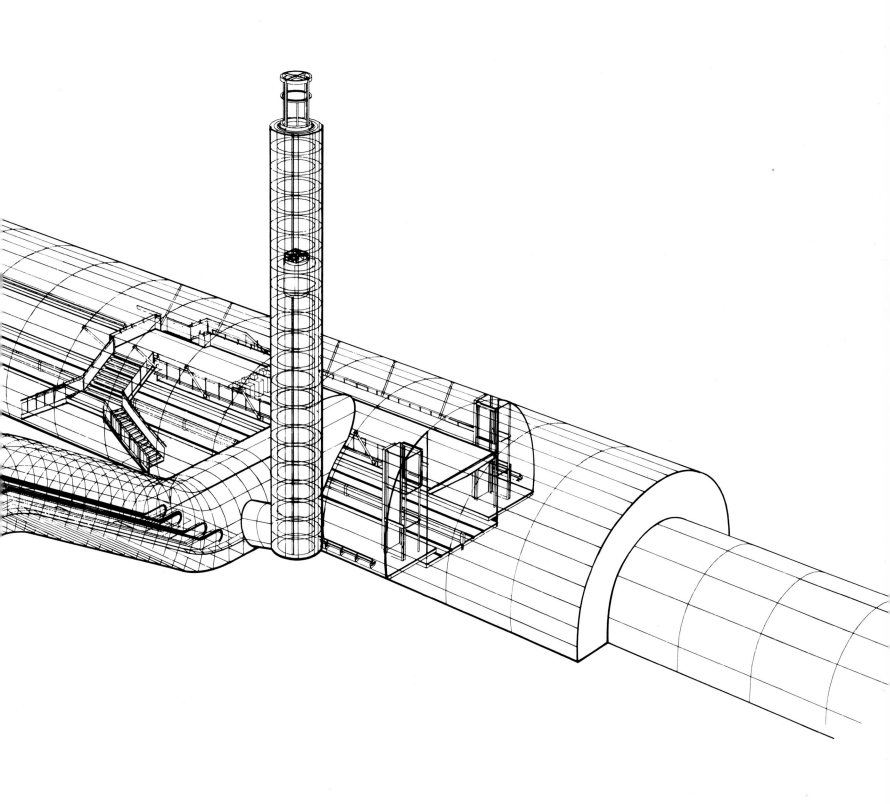

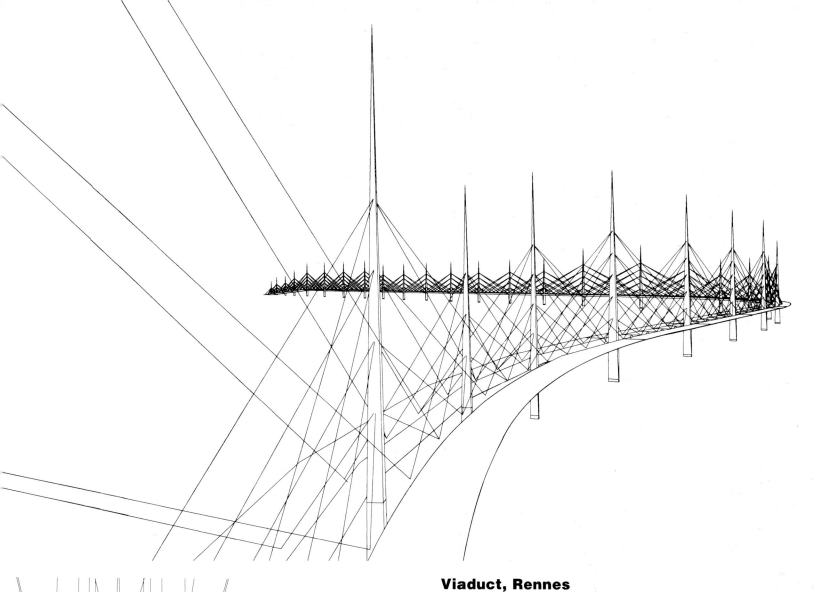

Viaduct, Rennes

*The modern inner-city viaduct –
usually an elevated route for a
rapid transit system or subway
railway – is seldom a thing of
beauty. Most are based on a
system of relatively massive
columns and beams, arranged at
uniform centres, irrespective of the
nature of the built environment
over, and through, which they
pass. The French city of Rennes
wanted a distinctive and high
quality viaduct for its VAL rapid
transit and sought a design
through limited competition. The
winning scheme, developed with
Ove Arup & Partners, is based
upon a kit consisting of four
elements: tall steel pylons; paired
suspension cables; precast
concrete deck units and steel
torsion links to support and link the
separate track structures and unite
the deck with the suspension
cables. These elements can be
combined into a continuous portal
structure (2,130m in length) with
spans of 20-50m.*

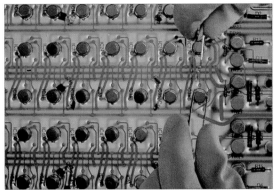

ENERGIE UND BELUEFTUNGS DIAGRAM
ENERGY AND AIR FLOW DIAGRAM

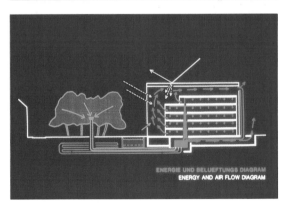

Electronic Park, Duisburg

Duisburg, at the heart of the Ruhr, is a city that in recent years has been subject to economic problems. The Electronic Park is a vital part of the city's regeneration.

The site is close to the city centre, on land once occupied by now-defunct industries. The layout has to be essentially urban, yet there is an obvious need for environmental improvement.

Foster Associates' masterplan accordingly devotes up to half the main site to public open spaces, to be planted with trees. The Micro Centre extends across Bismarkstrasse in the form of two climate halls, each 22m tall, containing 12 separate buildings targeted at electronics-based industries in a total space of 30,000sq m. The external envelope of the halls uses transparent insulation materials, special light-guiding systems, sun reflectors and heat collectors to create the optimum temperature. Air intakes set amongst the trees draw fresh air through underground pipes, cooling or warming it according to

the season. A water pool is also used to cool the building. The intention is to create an energy-saving environment that is controlled but not artificially serviced – in short, a 'green' building. Within the envelope, individual buildings can be serviced according to the specific needs of users. It is hoped to start on the climate halls early in 1992.

Two other buildings are under construction: the eye-catching Business Promotion Centre is eight storeys high and 4,000sq m in area, with an exhibition hall, conference facilities and offices. A sophisticated triple insulating skin provides maximum user comfort. The Telematic Centre is a market place for the region. Its circular drum provides a new focus for the inner-city area.

__Above__: Duisburg was once dominated by traditional heavy industries – now declining in importance. __Centre above__: The city's growth industries are rooted in electronics and information technologies. __Centre below__: Foster's scheme is energy conscious and environment-friendly. __Below__: Water and trees provide a green setting for new buildings.

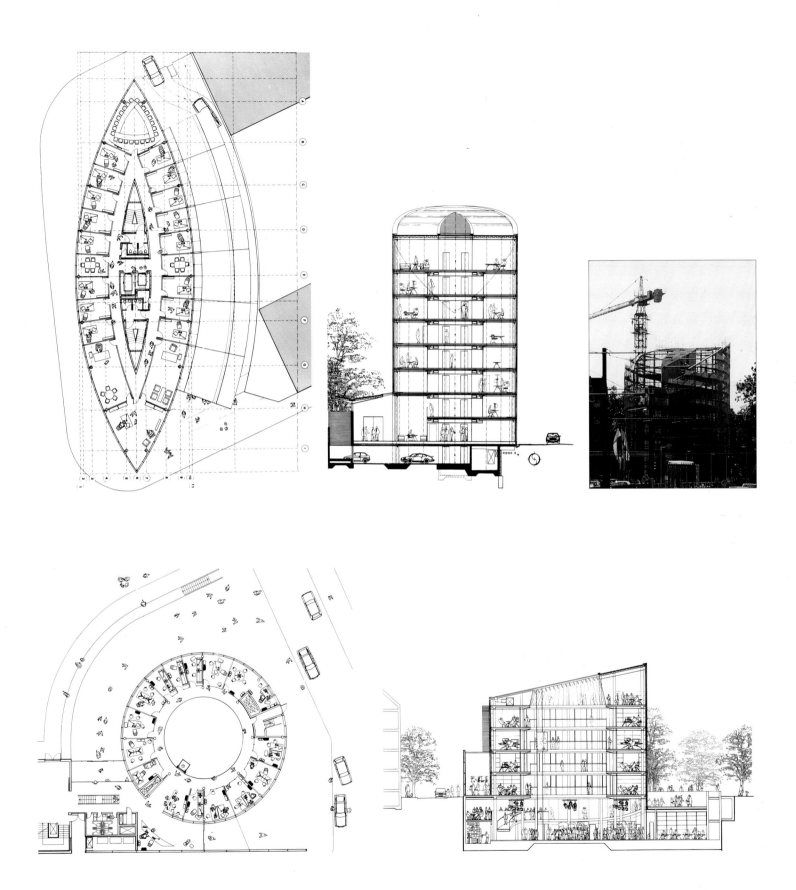

Technical Park, Toulouse

With a total area of some 20,000m sq, the Fonta scheme is the largest office development in the Labège Technical Park on the outskirts of Toulouse. The scheme consists of eight individual buildings, designed to be constructed in phases. The base unit is a block of cellular offices covering 100m sq, which may be combined to form one back-to-back block. The blocks are linked to each other by service lift and staircase towers to form double, triple and quadruple units, butted together to form a series of linked roofs and protected internal courtyards. The scheme thus grows by increments, but from the motorway that fringes the site it reads as a unified whole.

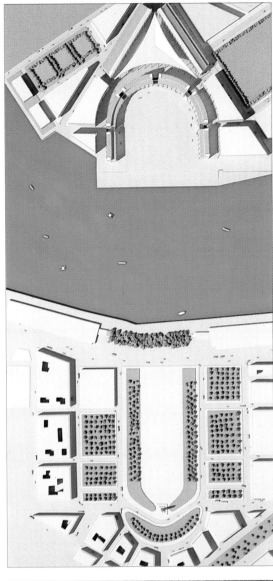

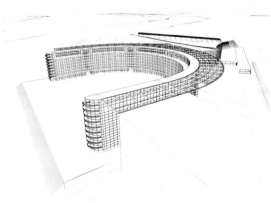

Mixed-Use Development, La Bastide, Bordeaux

At Bordeaux, Foster confronted head-on the work of an architect whose philosophy of design could not be more different from his own. The Catalan Classicist Ricardo Bofill had been commissioned by the city to masterplan the Bastide area, which lies across the river Gironde from the city centre.

Bofill always favours grand gestures in the Beaux-Arts tradition – and the French have allowed his predilections free rein at Montpellier and elsewhere – but there was some excuse for this approach along the Bordeaux riverside (which looks across to the magnificent Place des Quinconces, one of the largest squares in all Europe). Foster Associates, in the event, inherited the basic plan of the project – a huge crescent, facing the river, with a large trade centre block behind – from the Bofill masterplan. The scheme responds admirably to the challenge and the opportunities of this fine site, while being recognisably and

distinctly a Foster product.

The crescent is comparable in scale to the Royal Crescent in Bath; the place it encloses, to the Campo in Siena. From the latter, it derives the idea of being gently dished, with shops and restaurants at ground-floor level and routes, in the form of galleria, cut through the buildings for pedestrian access. A continuous galleria runs behind the crescent, separating office buildings and exhibition halls. The original planning permission was signifi-cantly modified to provide for Foster's conception, which tempers grandeur with a concern for human scale and public amenity which is not, alas, always found in Bofill's work.

The detailed treatment of the buildings is one hundred percent Foster – cool, elegant, incisive, with a sophisticated use of glass throughout. The Bastide scheme, a straightforward commercial project and subject to commercial constraints on cost, is likely to give this remarkable historic city a new dimension which extends far beyond a mere reworking of historicist themes.

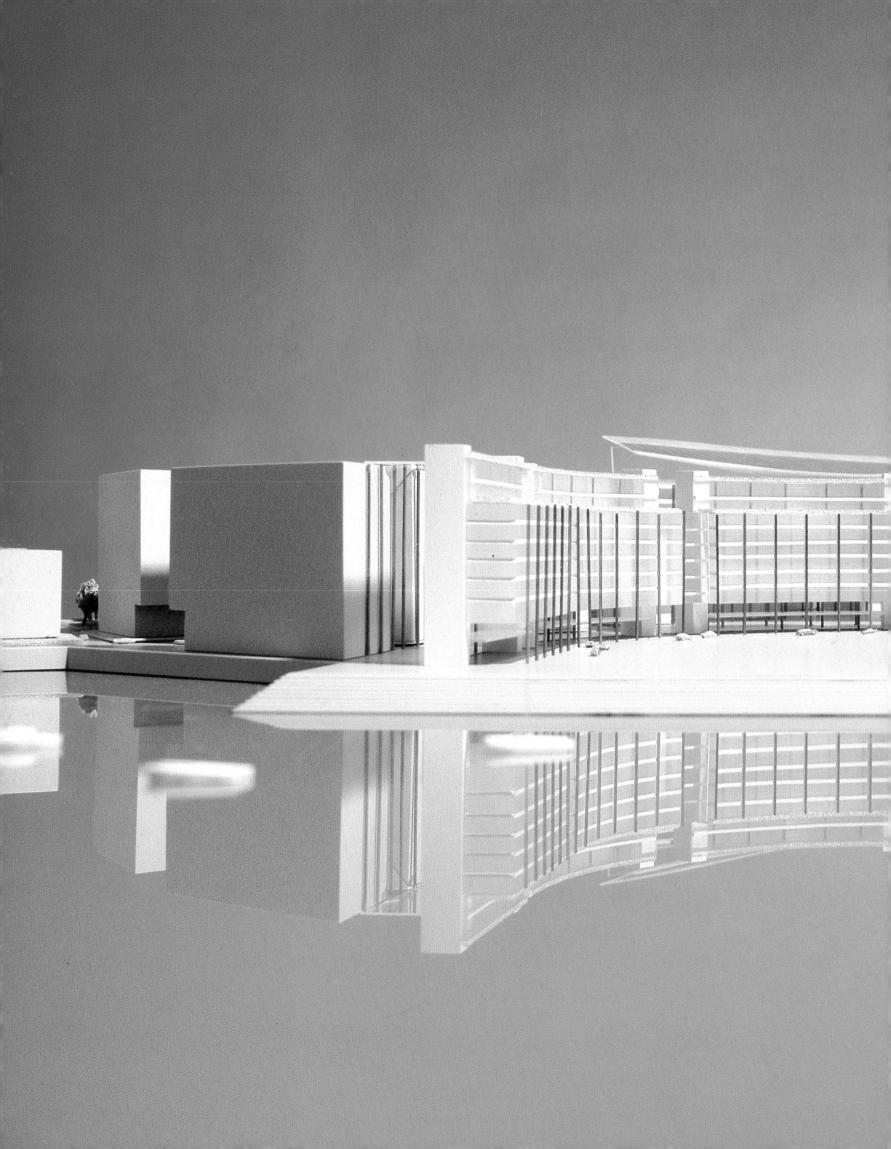

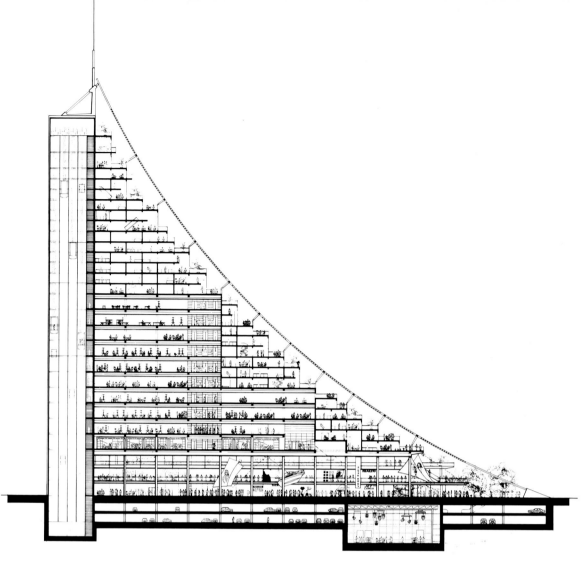

Mixed-Use Development, Shinagawa, Tokyo

This scheme, which has a total gross area of 31,500sq m, is proposed for a waterfront site in the Shinagawa district of Tokyo Harbour.

The building tapers in section with apartments cascading down the southern elevation in stepped roof terraces. The lower floors contain restaurants, shops and cafes. A radio station incorporating six broadcasting studios sits above these at the heart of the building. The height of the structure is determined by the need for high transmitters and radio masts and also for a studio overlooking the harbour. The residential roof terraces are shaded by a louvered and glazed roof which sweeps down the southern elevation in an uninterrupted concave curve.

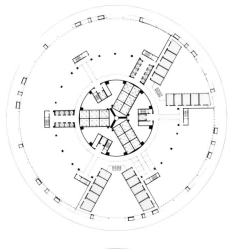

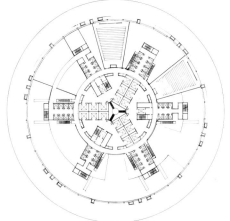

Millennium Tower, Tokyo

At 840m, the proposed Millennium Tower will be almost twice the height of Sears Tower, currently the world's tallest building. It will resemble a small township, with a resident population of 50,000 and the mixture of work and leisure activities that might be found in a major city thoroughfare like New York's Fifth Avenue or Tokyo's Ginza. The tower itself will be 130m diameter at its base and will occupy an enclosed 400m diameter marina. Sky centres are located every 30 floors, providing identity and scale for the huge edifice, and accommodating communal facilities. In between, there will be a mixture of activities, ranging from commercial and professional services of all kinds, to manufacture and assembly as well as residential around segmental atria. High-speed lifts capable of carrying up to 150 people run up inside the tower's helical steel structure and serve the sky centres. From here, the visitor completes his journey by means of conventional high-speed lifts.

113

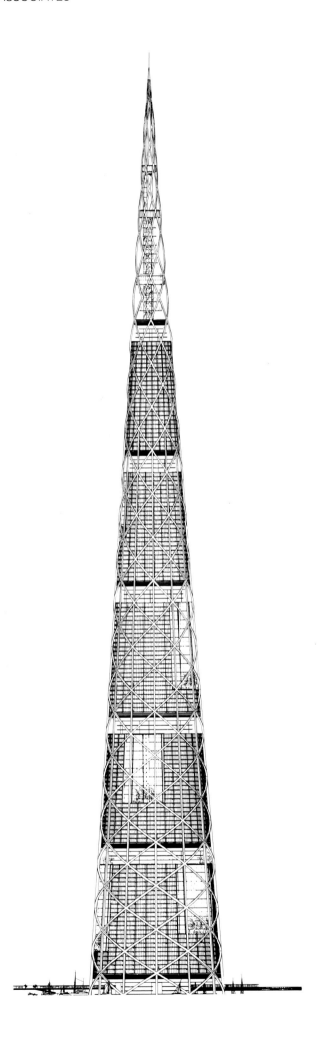

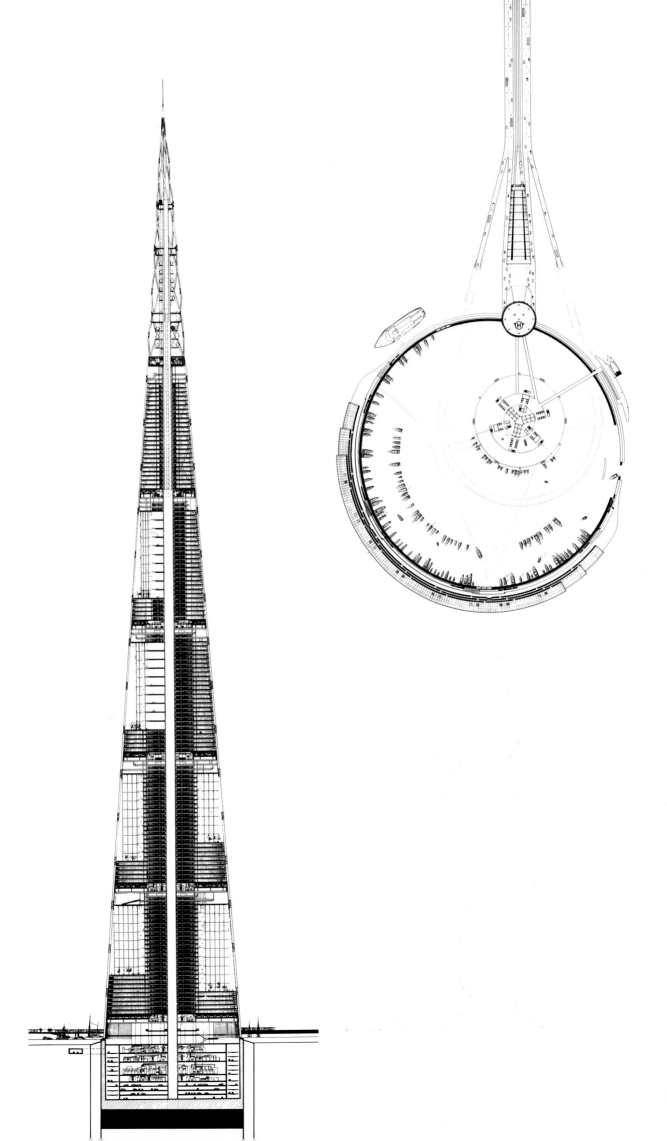

Industrial Design, Street Furniture

Street furniture can easily become street litter. The standard local authority litter bin is a proliferating species, and in some ways as unsightly as the litter it is supposed to collect. The guiding principle behind the range of units designed for Stansted was simplicity. An unobtrusive family of objects was devised – bollards, illuminated bollards and litter bins – using primary forms to match the language of the terminal structure. All units are in grey metal, with concealed fixings.

On a larger scale, the practice has developed for the French firm J-C Decaux a bus shelter system based on two structural poles and glass panels, and also an aggrandised version of the Colonne Morris – a rotating advertising drum with an elliptical attachment which could incorporate grit bins, benches, lavatories, a roof canopy and electronic information systems.

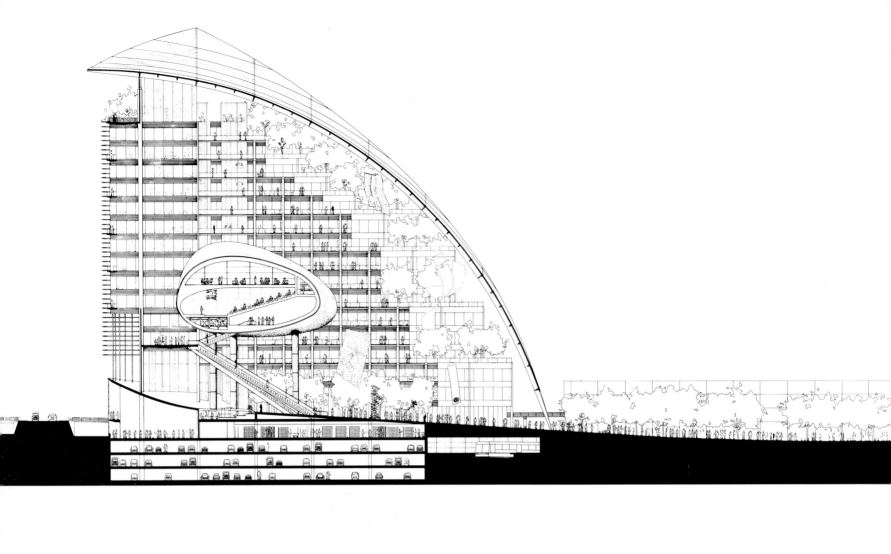

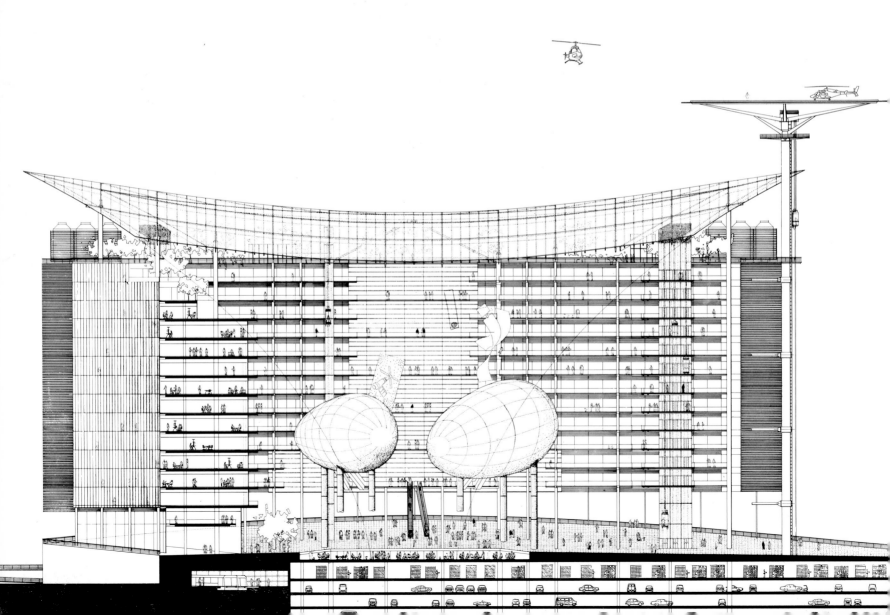

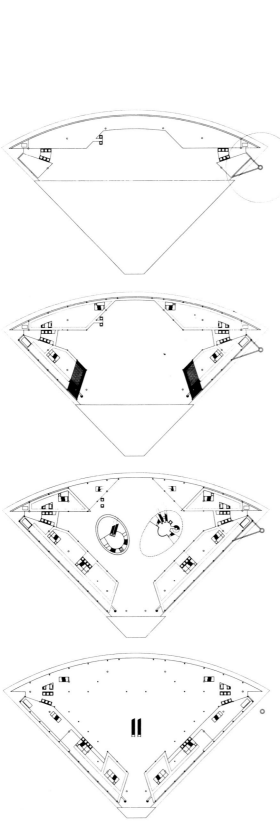

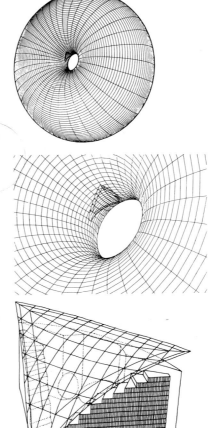

Hôtel du Département, Marseilles

The Ville de Marseilles set up an international competition for their new regional government head-quarters, a building which was to be not only an important meeting point for the community, but also a symbol of the region and the city.

The building designed was a unique response to a very special challenge, as it had to work both from the outside, as a powerful image of regional government, and from the inside, as a work-place, a meeting place and a place to visit.

Internally, the architectural form of the auditorium and the debating chambers is of suspended shiny ovoids. Each individual part of the building is given a specific identity, whether it is for housing elected council members, the public or general office workers, and these elements all come together around a dramatic internal space.

The elegant, low-energy concept for the building is a direct response to the local climate and *the restrictions of the site. The design was also sensitive to local construction capabilities, being very simple and inexpensive and based on tried and tested methods of construction to produce a very economical solution.*

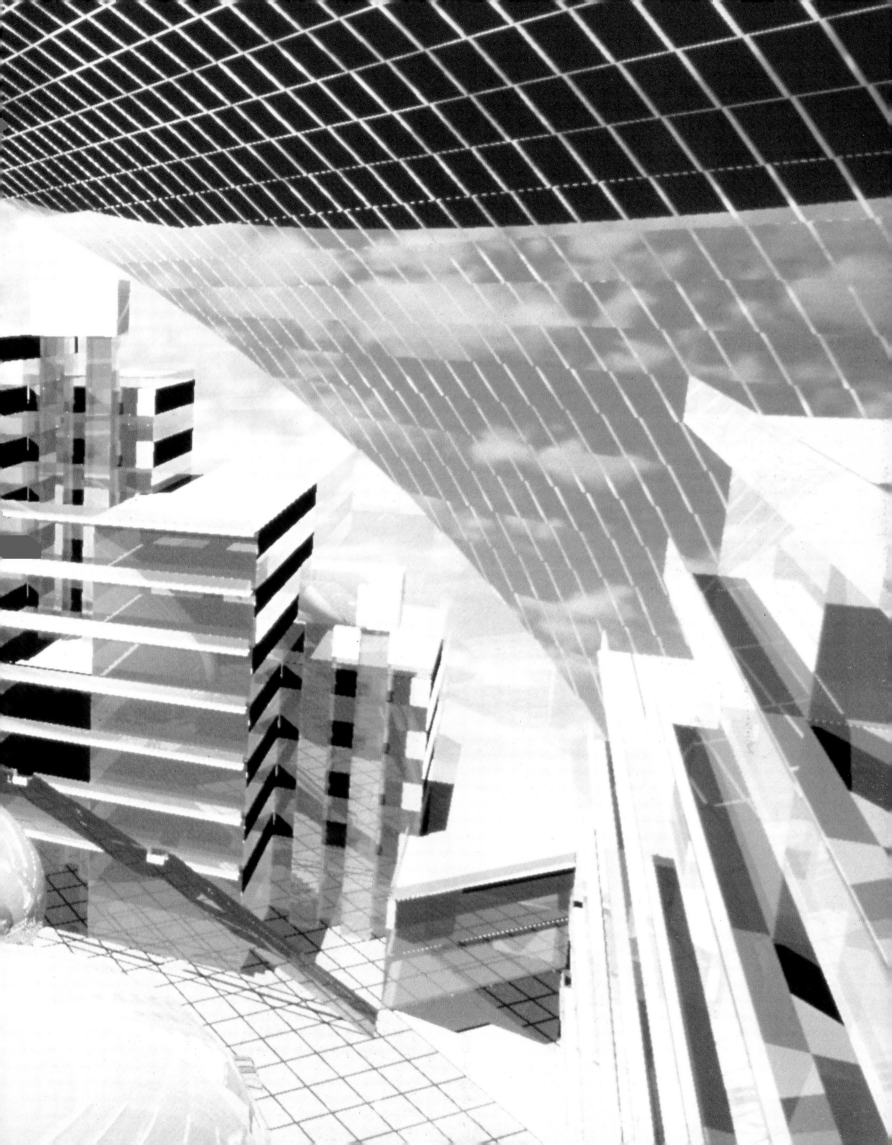

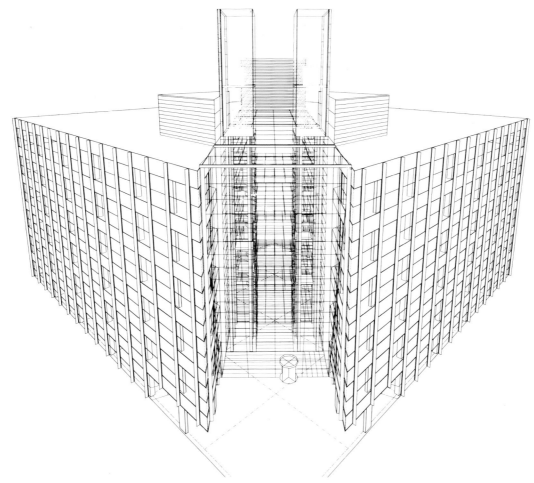

Offices, Chiswick Park, London

Industrial and technical parks are usually found on city fringes. Chiswick Park, a joint development by Stanhope Properties and Trafalgar House, brings planned commercial development much closer to the city centre. The overall site is the size of Berkeley Square. The developers' masterplan has been conceived as a formal square with a number of architects taking responsibility for the different buildings. The Foster Associates scheme is square on plan, with an atrium cutting through on the diagonal. Both sections have views over the park and are linked to one another across the atrium by bridges and catwalks.

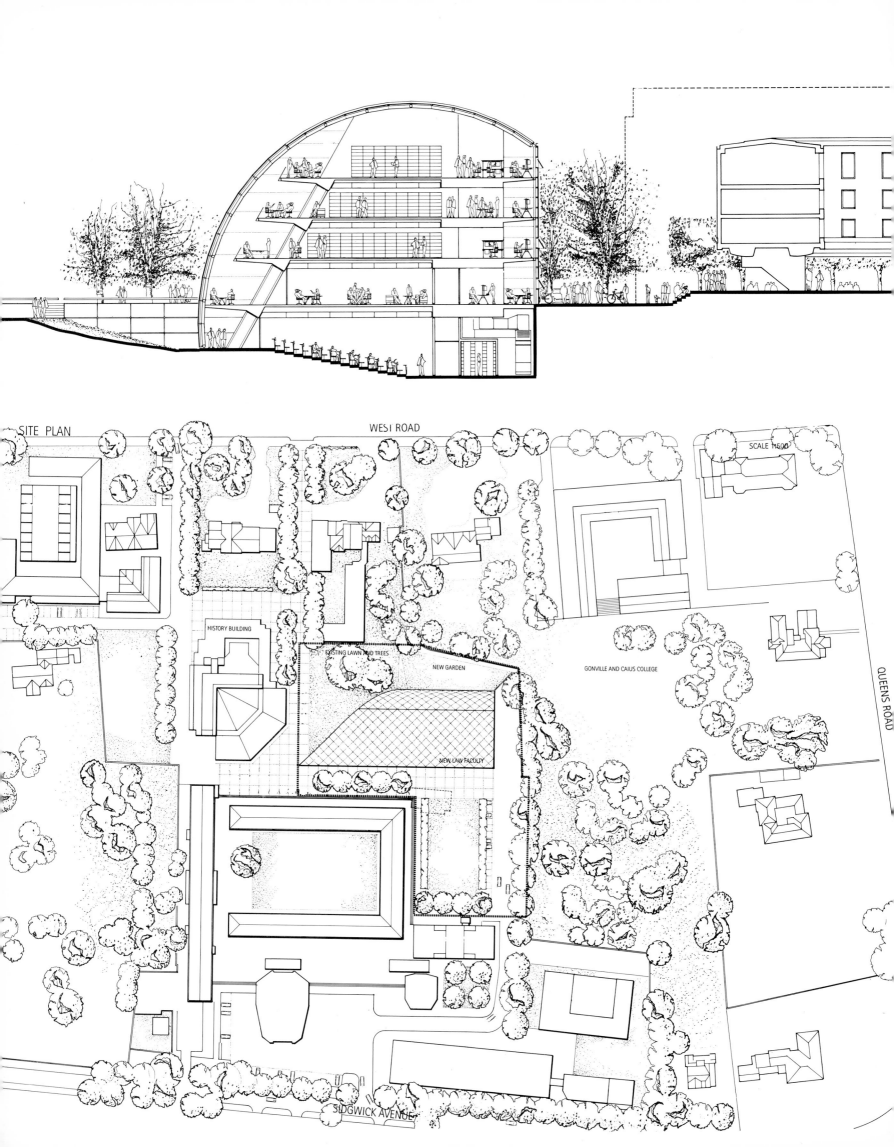

SITE PLAN

WEST ROAD

SCALE 1:500

HISTORY BUILDING

EXISTING LAWN AND TREES

NEW GARDEN

GONVILLE AND CAIUS COLLEGE

NEW LAW FACULTY

QUEENS ROAD

SIDGWICK AVENUE

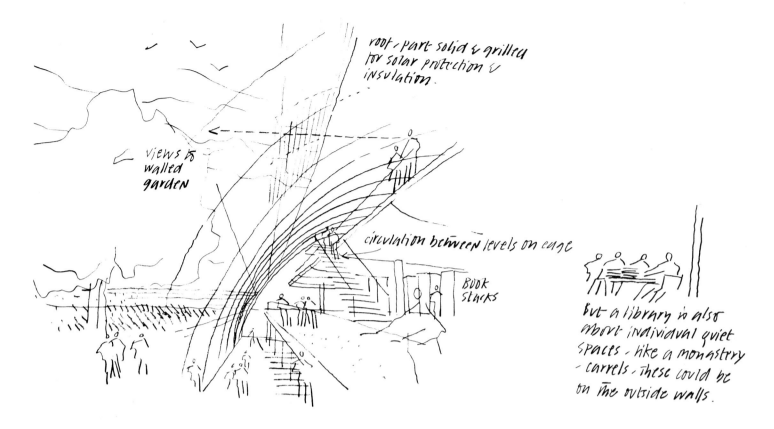

roof, part solid & grilled
for solar protection &
insulation.

views to
walled
garden

circulation between levels on edge

BOOK
stacks

But a library is also
about individual quiet
spaces - like a monastery
- carrels. These could be
on the outside walls.

The proposals are diagrammatic - a statement of intent - some thoughts for _discussion_ & development.

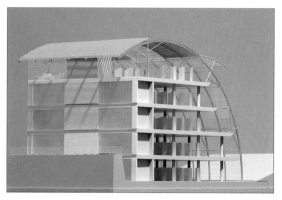

Law Faculty, Cambridge University

Academically and architecturally, the Sidgwick Avenue site and the area immediately around it at Cambridge University are of great interest and importance. The faculty buildings and graduate halls of residence comprise an anthology of post-war British architecture including lecture theatres, libraries and faculty buildings by Casson Conder & Partners, the History Faculty library by James Stirling, and Harvey Court, designed by Leslie Martin. Between these, in the garden of 7 West Road, the Law Faculty and the Institute of Criminology plan to combine their existing facilities in a new, four-storey pavilion is due for completion in 1994 and will include a library, lecture rooms and study areas. The building is wedge shaped on plan with entrance and reception at its sharp end, dense bookstacks arranged in a flexible central space and study areas lit by natural light. The clear glazed roof line runs in an uninterrupted curve down to the lower ground floor on the garden side, giving magnificent views of lawns and mature trees.

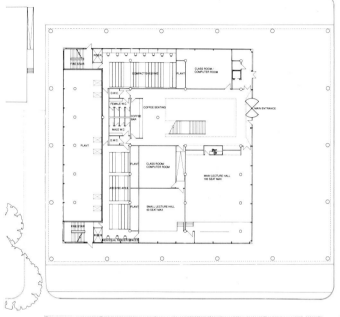

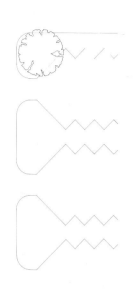

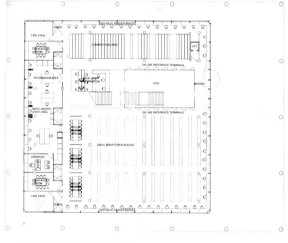

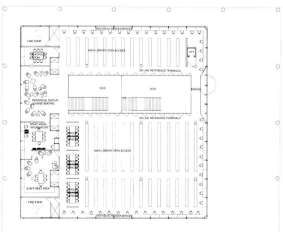

Cranfield Institute Library, Bedfordshire

Foster's new library at Cranfield Institute of Technology will serve an institution devoted to the training of technologists and managers and will bring together the resources of two libraries, presently housed in separate buildings. The Institute started life in 1946 as a school of aeronautical engineering – so that the design, evoking the architecture of aircraft hangars with its great vaulted roofs, has a particular relevance.

The library will be located at the centre of the campus, providing it with a new focus. (A generous canopy, as at Nîmes, suggests the possibility of outdoor events here.) It is designed to cater for a high level of information technology – every Cranfield student is equipped with a personal computer as a matter of course. Flexible desks are intended to cater for an intensive power and data access: this is not a conventional library.

The look of the new building reflects this. Clad in steel and glass on a concrete frame – exposed on the interiors – it makes optimum use of natural light, while a louvred colonnade reduces glare at the perimeter. Inside, the main stairs will be steel framed, with a glass balustrade. The balcony to the edge of the atrium will be formed of single sheets of cantilevered toughened glass.

This is a tough logical building for a school devoted to technical and business progress. Foster, however, imbues it with a poetry which reflects his own optimistic – if critical – view of technology and progress.

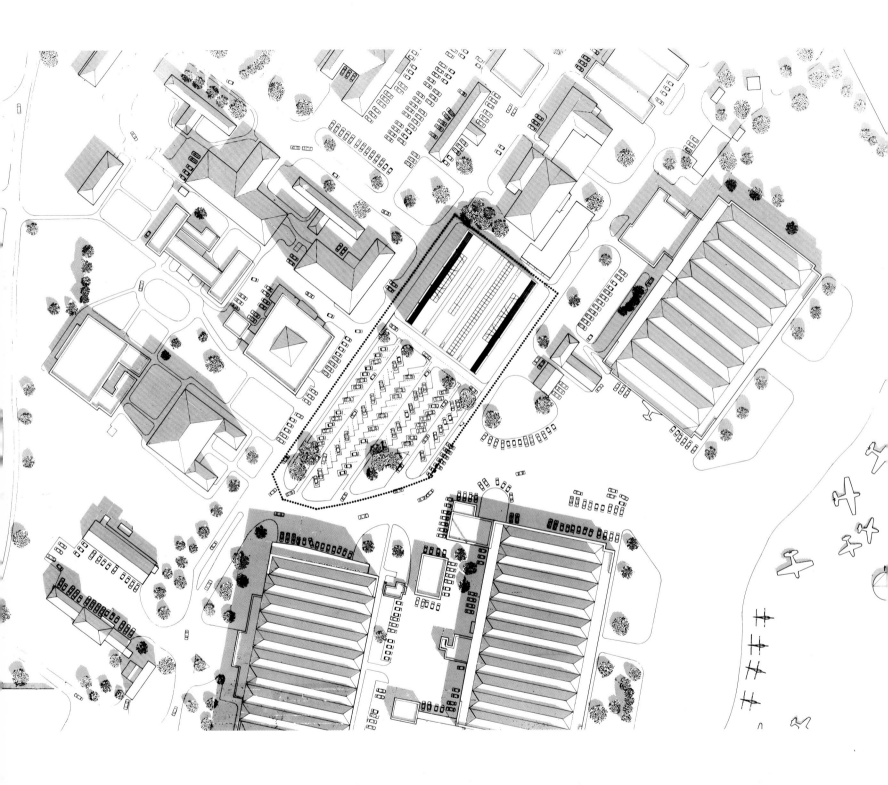

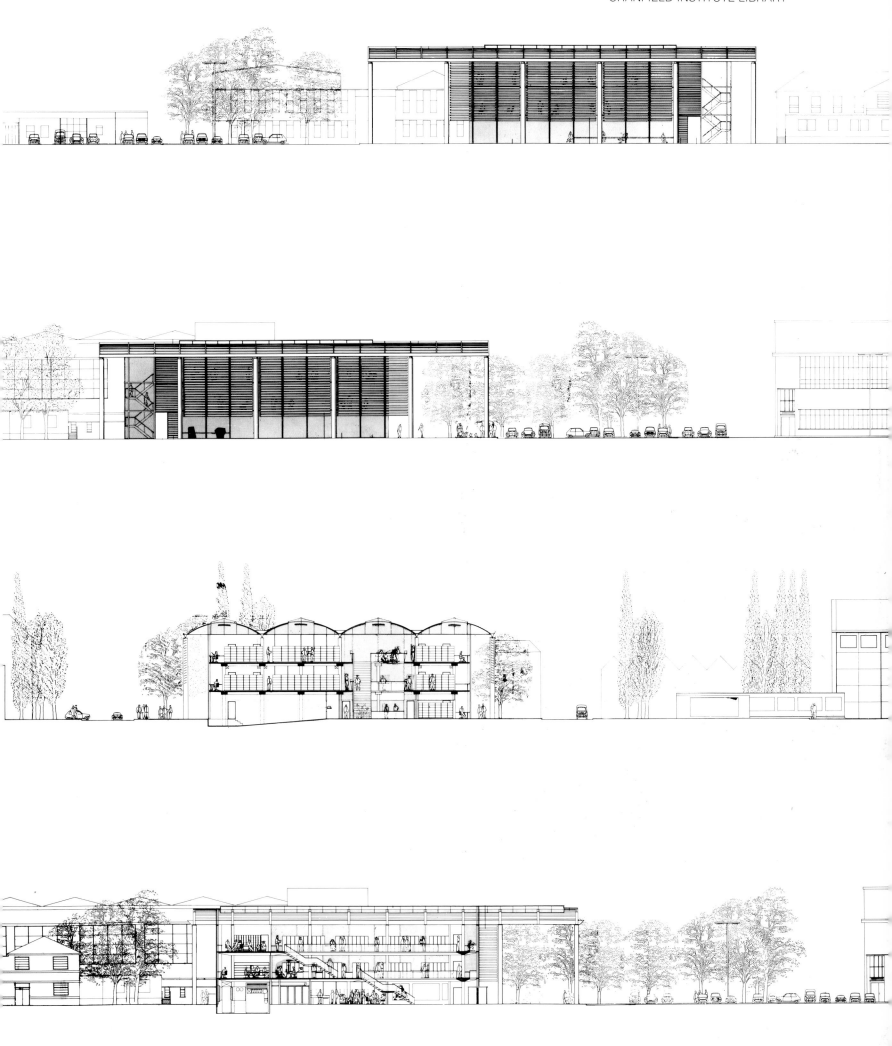

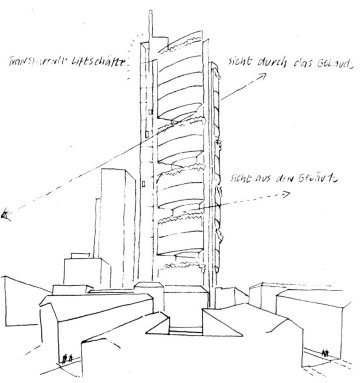

Transparente Liftschafte

sicht durch das Gebaude,

sicht aus den Gebaute

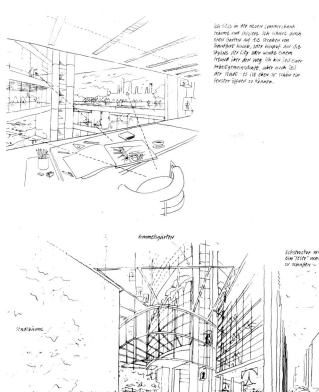

Commerzbank Headquarters, Frankfurt am Main

Foster Associates' success in the competition for a new headquarters for Commerzbank at the centre of Frankfurt is a decisive step in the practice's move towards increasingly ecologically sophisticated buildings.

The Bank, like other major German businesses, embraces 'green' policies wholeheartedly. It currently occupies a number of buildings spread around Frankfurt, with its principal offices in a 70's tower behind Kaiserplatz. The new building will adjoin the latter, with provision made in the scheme for its possible eventual replacement.

Norman Foster has always regretted that the 'garden in the sky' planned for the Hongkong Bank failed to materialise; at Frankfurt, he has been able to return to the theme and to adopt a system of natural air conditioning which would have been inconceivable in the Hongkong Bank.

The form of the block is triangular with three 'petals' of office floors spreading out from a central stem up which a central slot provides cooling draughts to all floors. Large fans draw in additional air when needed. Every third floor, the offices are interspersed with gardens staggered around the height of the tower, so that every office has a view into a garden. In a tower of this height, conventional opening windows are impractical but windows have been designed to open behind a wind-break layer of glazing.

All this is made possible by a well-conceived structural form, providing clear-span spaces with six-storey units suspended from the basic structure.

At ground level, the building sits amidst a huddle of 19th-century blocks. A new glazed courtyard will be open to the public, with gardens and restaurants, as an alternative to the usual tower-in-piazza formula.

The detailed designs for Commerzbank will concentrate on heightening the sense of identity and place in the building, one set to become the first of the big 'green' office buildings of the late 20th century.

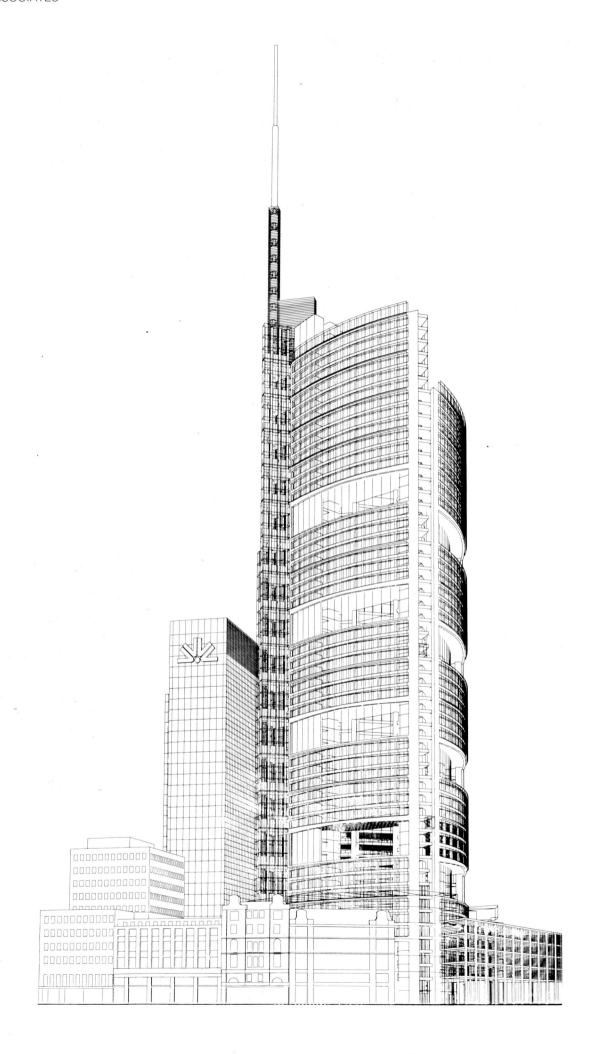

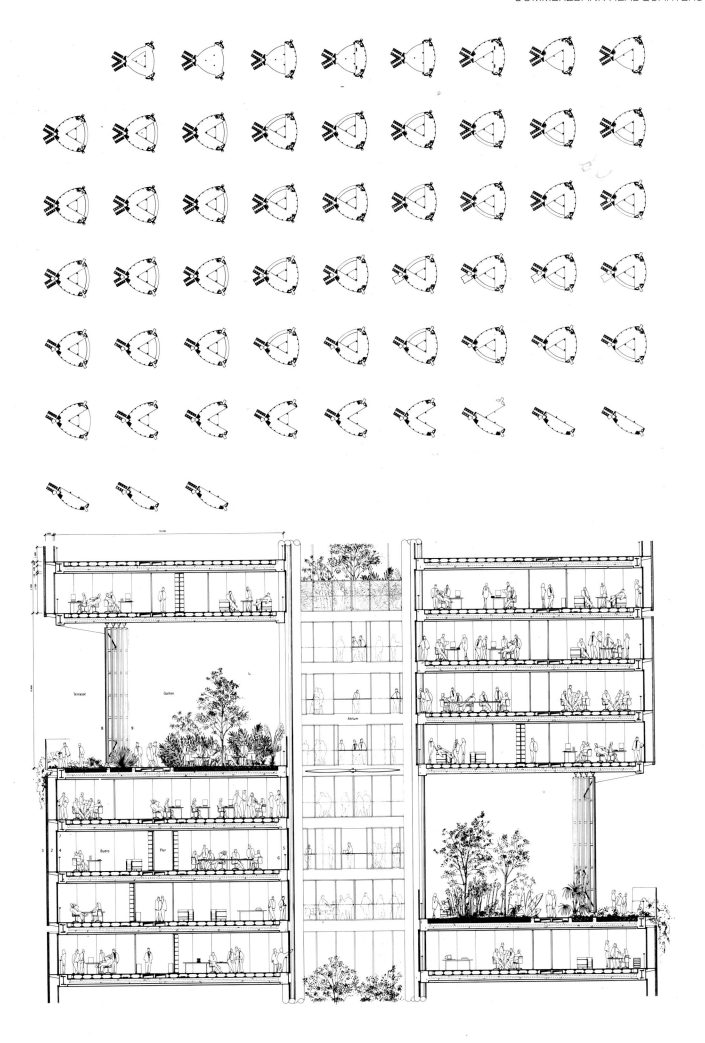

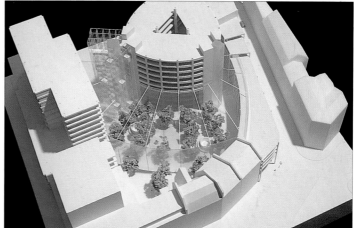

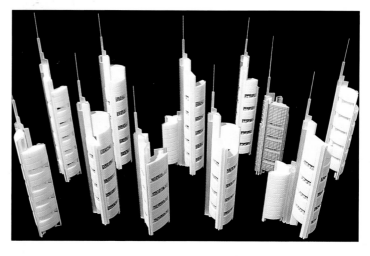

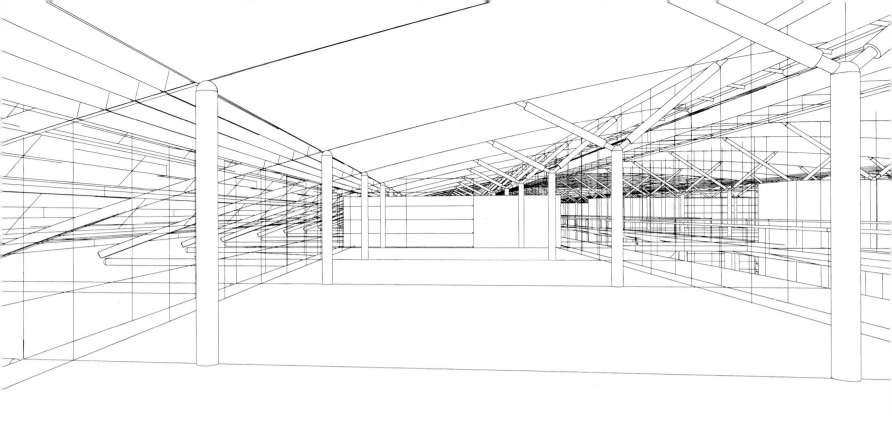

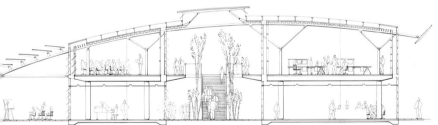

Deuxième Lycée Polyvalent Régional, Fréjus

The commission to Foster Associates to design a new school at Fréjus in the south of France reflects Norman Foster's immense personal admiration for the French and for their commitment to good public architecture as well as his close interest in education. The scheme also embodies many of the environmental and ecological concerns which are now a preoccupation of the practice.

The building has to be moderate in cost and quick to build – it provides for the expanding population of this southern boom-town and is scheduled to open in the autumn of 1993. The school will house over 900 students, including an element of vocational training which demands work-shops and other specialised spaces.

The site straddles a hill, with fine views out towards the sea and hills. The building has to cope with the hot climate – the experience of Nîmes was useful here – but air conditioning was proposed. The structure utilises the 'solar chimney' effect, employing hot air to draw in cool air in a manner common in traditional Arabic architecture.

The internal arrangement, along a 'street' with classrooms opening off and service centres at 33m intervals, is in tune with the social ideals of the institution and marks a return to school architecture for Foster, whose unexecuted Newport scheme (1967) undoubtedly influenced the schools built recently in Hampshire under Colin Stansfield-Smith. (Queen's Inclosure Middle School is one that Foster especially admires.)

Externally, the building is rooted in the landscape by the use of tree-planting, with the tree forms echoing the sweep of the roof.

The school will be a fine example of moderately priced, easily constructed public building of the sort which Foster would like to see more of in Britain. Very simple and repetitive, it derives its special qualities from a rigorous plan and careful attention to detail. It provides an exemplar for the future public domain.

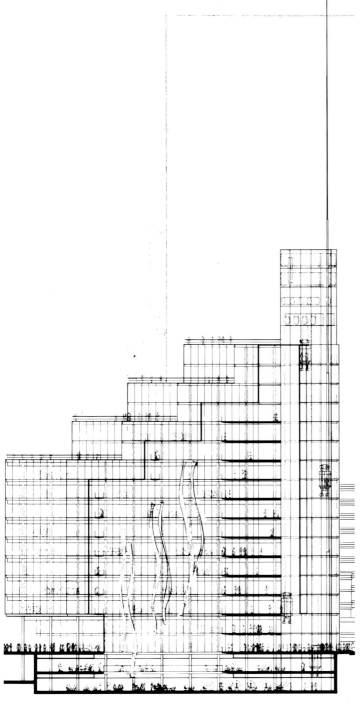

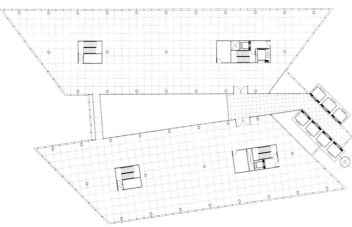

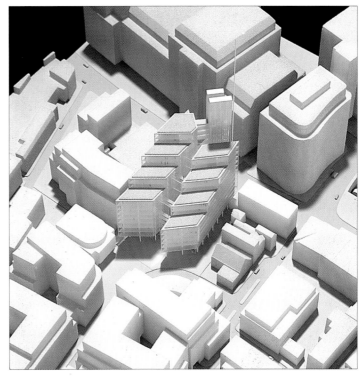

Spitalfields Development, London

Spitalfields Market, one of the oldest wholesale markets in London, closed in May 1991, leaving a 12-acre site vacant. To the west is Liverpool Street Station, a busy commuter terminus, and the huge Broadgate office development, a product of the 80s, with large, Post-Modernist slabs lining Bishopsgate. To the east is the Spitalfields area, with streets of early Georgian houses and Hawksmoor's Christ Church.

Foster's brief was to create a 'landmark' building on the western edge of the site which includes 1.1 million sq ft of offices and 100 shops, plus restaurants, cafes and 165 apartments. The building is a gateway to the scheme and has to stand up to the overbearing frontages opposite. It could also be seen as a symbol of a new direction in City architecture, away from the Post-Modernist fancies of the 80s and back to the enterprising spirit which created Lloyd's. Spitalfields is likely to be Foster's first City of London building.

The tower has to respect the scale of the new 'Bishop's Square', surrounded by far lower blocks. It is therefore stepped down as it moves east. Potentially, this requirement could give the block a jagged look, but all-over glazed canopies restore the equilibrium. Concentrating services in the basements and placing lifts in a dramatic tower obviates the need for clumsy services in boxes on the roofs. The latter therefore become open galleries, accessible to office users.

This is a developer's building which has to meet a strict budget, without sacrificing quality. The office floors are relatively straightforward, but far more appealing as workplaces than the overpowering expanses of Broadgate. Foster addresses the issue of public amenity by creating a lofty galleria, open at all hours, which slices through the building.

The tower will be finished in steel and glass panels, culminating in a steel mast 140m tall. At Spitalfields, Foster has addressed the problem of commercial architecture, producing a design of dramatic distinction.

PRINCIPAL PROJECTS

1991	Commerzbank headquarters, Frankfurt
1991	Gateway office building, Spitalfields Development, London
1991	Deuxième Lycée Polyvalent Regional (Secondary School), Fréjus
1991	University of Cambridge Institute of Criminology, Cambridge
1991	Office building for Stanhope Properties and County Natwest, Holborn, London
1991	New headquarters and retail building for Sanaei Corp, Makuhari, Japan
1991	New headquarters for Agiplan, Mulheim, Germany
1991	New headquarters for Obunsha Corp, Yarai Cho, Tokyo
1991	Imperial War Museum Exhibition Hangar, Duxford, Essex
1991	Canary Wharf Station for the Jubilee Line underground extension
1991	Viaduct, Rennes
1990	Masterplan for Berlin
1990	Masterplan for Cannes
1990	Masterplan for Nîmes
1990	Law Faculty, Cambridge University
1990	Office building for Fonta, Toulouse
1990	Competition for Hôtel du Département, Marseilles
1990	Competition for Congress Hall, San Sebastian, Spain
1990	Competition for Trade Fair Centre, Berlin
1990	Offices for Stanhope Properties, London Wall, London
1989	Passenger Concourse building for British Rail, King's Cross, London
1989-1991	Offices for Stanhope Properties, Chiswick Park Development, London
1989-1992	New library for Cranfield Institute of Technology, Bedfordshire
1989	Planning studies for Cambridge
1989-1994	Office building DS2 at Canary Wharf, Docklands, London
1989	Street furniture for Decaux, Paris
1989-1991	British Rail station, Stansted Airport, Essex
1989	Technology Centres, Edinburgh and Glasgow
1989	Office building for Jacob's Island Co, Docklands, London
1988-1990	ITN headquarters, Holborn, London
1988-	Technology Centre and Business Promotion Centre, Duisburg
1988-	Sackler Galleries, Jerusalem
1988-1991	Crescent Wing, Sainsbury Centre for the Visual Arts, UEA, Norwich
1988-1991	Telecommunications Tower, Torre di Collserola, Barcelona
1988-1993	Metro Railway system, Bilbao
1988	Shop for Esprit, Knightsbridge, London
1988	Contract carpet and tile design for Vorwerk
1988	Pont d'Austerlitz bridge across the Seine, Paris
1988	Offices for Stanhope Securities, City of London
1988	Holiday Inn, The Hague
1987-	King's Cross masterplan, London
1987-1989	Riverside housing and light industrial complex, Hammersmith, London
1987-1991	Century Tower office building, Bunkyo-ku, Tokyo
1987-	Kawana House, Japan
1987-1989	Offices for Stanhope Securities, Stockley Park, Uxbridge, Middlesex
1987	Competition for Turin Airport
1987	Hotel for La Fondiaria, Florence
1987	Shopping Centre for Savacentre near Southampton
1987	Bunka Radio Station, Yarai Cho, Tokyo
1987	Competition for Paternoster Square redevelopment, London
1986-1990	Riverside offices and apartments, Chelsea Reach, London
1986	Salle de Spectacles, Nancy
1986	Headquarters for Televisa, Mexico City
1986	Shop for Katharine Hamnett

1985-1991	The Sackler Galleries, Royal Academy of Arts, London
1985-1987	Furniture system for Tecno, Milan
1985	New offices for IBM at Greenford, Middlesex
1984-1992	Centre d'Art Contemporain et Médiathèque, Carré d'Art, Nîmes
1984-1986	IBM Head Office, major refit, Cosham, Hampshire
1982-1985	New Radio Centre for BBC, London
1982	Autonomous Dwelling (with Buckminster Fuller), USA
1982	Competition for Headquarters of Humana Inc, Louisville, Kentucky
1981	Foster Associates office, Great Portland Street, London
1981	Internal Systems, Furniture for Foster Associates
1981-1986	National Indoor Athletics Stadium, Frankfurt, Germany
1981-1991	Third London Airport Stansted, Essex:
	New Terminal Building
	New Airside Satellites
	Landside Airside Coach Stations
	Terminal Zone Masterplan
1981	Competition for Billingsgate Fish Market, London
1980-1983	Parts Distribution Centre for Renault UK Ltd, Swindon, Wiltshire
1980	Planning Studies for Statue Square, Hong Kong
1980	Students' Union Building, University College, London
1979-1986	New Headquarters for the Hongkong Bank, Hong Kong
1979	Granada Entertainment Centre, Milton Keynes
1979	Shop for Joseph, Knightsbridge, London
1978	London Gliding Club, Dunstable Downs
1978-1979	Foster Residence, Hampstead, London
1978	Proposals for International Energy Expo, Knoxville, USA
1978	Open House Community Project, Cwmbran, Wales
1978	Whitney Museum Development Project, New York
1977-1979	Technical Park for IBM, Rockware Avenue, Greenford, Middlesex
1977-1979	Transportation Interchange for LTE, Hammersmith, London
1976-1977	Masterplan for St Helier Harbour, Jersey
1975-1976	Regional Planning Studies for Island of Gomera, Canaries
1975	Fred Olsen Gate Redevelopment, Oslo, Norway
1974-1978	Sainsbury Centre for Visual Arts, UEA, Norwich, Norfolk
1974-1975	Palmerston Special School, Liverpool
1974	Country Club and Marina, Son, Norway
1974	Travel Agency for Fred Olsen Ltd, London
1974	Offices for Fred Olsen Ltd, Vestby, Norway
1973-1975	Low Rise Housing, Bean Hill, Milton Keynes Development Corporation
1973-1974	Headquarters for VW Audi NSU and Mercedes Benz, Milton Keynes
1973-1977	Aluminium Extrusion Plant for SAPA, Tibshelf, Derby
1972-1973	Orange Hand Boys Wear Shops for Burton Group
1972-1973	Modern Art Glass Ltd, Thamesmead, Kent
1971-1975	Willis Faber and Dumas Head Office, Greyfriars, Ipswich, Suffolk
1971-1973	Special Care Unit, Ickborough Road, Hackney, London
1971	Foster Associates Studio, London
1971	Theatre for St Peter's College, Oxford
1971	Climatroffice
1971-1972	Retail and Leisure Studies, Liverpool, Exeter and Badhoevedorp
1970-1971	Fred Olsen Ltd Passenger Terminal, Millwall
1970-1971	Computer Technology Ltd, Hemel Hempstead, Hertfordshire
1970-1971	IBM Advance Head Office, Cosham, Hampshire
1970	Air-Supported Structure for Computer Technology Ltd, Hertfordshire
1969	Factory Systems Studies
1969	Masterplan for Fred Olsen Ltd, Millwall Docks
1968-1969	Fred Olsen Ltd Amenity Centre, Millwall
1967	Newport School Competition
1965-1966	Reliance Controls Ltd, Swindon, Wiltshire
1965	Housing for Wates, Coulsden
1965	Henrion Studio, London
1964	Forest Road Extension, East Horsley, Surrey
1964	Mews Houses, Murray Mews, Camden Town, London
1964	Waterfront Housing, Cornwall
1964-1966	Skybreak House, Radlett, Hertfordshire
1964-1966	Creek Vean House, Feock, Cornwall
1964	Cockpit, Cornwall